Kate's
KITCHEN

ISBN 9 798870 719238

Written by Kate Healey-Stapleton.
Designed by Joanna Humphrey.

LEGS, BUMS & BUBBAS!

www.legsbumsandbubbas.com

🅾 kate_fitness.for.mums

f Legs, Bums & Bubbas

CONTENTS

Breakfast

Lunch

 Dairy Free

 Gluten Free

 Vegetarian

 Prep time

 Servings

Dinner

Savoury Snacks

Sweets Treats

A note from Kate

When you mention food, especially as a fitness mum, most people sadly think of restriction, not eating certain foods, calories and maybe not even enjoying your food! I am soooo far from this!!!

I combine nutrition, healthy eating and something very unique, to bring you 100 utterly fabulous recipes. Each one will make your taste buds dance with delight!

With **Kate's Kitchen** you can:

FEEL	**ENJOY**	**TRUST**	**A BALANCED**
confident in the kitchen and enjoy eating impressive meals with your family	eating healthy food and showcase great relationships with food to your children	that you are filling your body with nutritional goodness without compromising on taste	diet will stop you feeling stuck with what to eat

All the while, working towards your body goals and becoming the healthiest and happiest version of you!

There are no 'cheats' to eating - there are no quick fixes to losing weight or developing better eating habits. It takes a little time to invest in finding the right food for your body, which you will enjoy and get excited about. So here I bring you **Kate's Kitchen**.

Healthy eating and cooking from scratch will no longer be a luxury, it will easily be part of your routine with my step by step recipes. You can feel more confident in the kitchen... and I have no doubt you will **WOW** your family and feel **EMPOWERED**!

This book has you covered with unique breakfast ideas to kick-start your day; speedy lunches to fill up on; impressive dinners for the family and of course high protein, nutritious snacks which you can prepare and have on hand to grab for when the cravings hit!

My approach is all about balance. From hearty salads and soups to comforting slow cooker meals, to restaurant quality family dinners and fun sweet treats, there is something to suit every palate and meet every dietary need.

I understand the need for recipes which not only provide essential nutrients, but also cater to various dietary preferences and restrictions. That's why you will find a variety of options, including gluten free, dairy free and vegetarian recipes. Plus quick, high protein and low calorie options too. I ensure that everyone can enjoy tasty and satisfying food.

So, welcome to my world of irresistible recipes, tailored specifically for you amazing mummies! Let me be your trusty companion with **Kate's Kitchen**. I am here to inspire you, and make your life in the kitchen easier and brighter.

Get ready for your eating habits to take an exciting boost and start feeling proud of what you are eating!

Let's do this ladies!

Kate
xxx

Breakfast

FLUFFY COTTAGE CHEESE PANCAKES

Sweet, moreish and high in protein!

 10 MINS **SERVES 4**

INGREDIENTS

For the pancakes:

4 eggs

200g cottage cheese

4 tbsp milk

2 tbsp honey + 2 tbsp extra for serving

1 tsp vanilla extract

150g all-purpose flour

1 tsp baking powder

½ tsp ground cinnamon

½ tsp salt

2 tbsp olive oil + 1 tbsp. for cooking

fresh berries for serving

METHOD

1   In a large bowl, whisk together the eggs, cottage cheese, milk, honey and vanilla extract. Sift in flour, baking powder, cinnamon and salt. Whisk until the flour is incorporated.

2   Now whisk in 2 tablespoons of the olive oil, and set the batter aside to rest for 10 minutes.

3   When ready to cook, lightly grease a large frying pan with olive oil and place over a medium heat. When the pan is hot, add the batter, roughly ¼ cup per pancake. Cook the pancakes for 2-3 minutes on each side.

4   Serve the pancakes warm, topped with fresh berries and a drizzle of honey.

CALORIES
415

CARBS
51G

PROTEIN
14G

FAT
18G

PEANUT BUTTER BANANA OVERNIGHT OATS

Simply dreamy and packed with protein to jump start your day!

 5 MINS SERVES 4

INGREDIENTS

2 bananas

3 tbsp smooth peanut butter

85g maple syrup

2 tsp vanilla extract

600ml almond milk unsweetened (or any milk of choice)

200g oats

2 tbsp chia seeds

METHOD

1   To a large mixing bowl, add the mashed banana together with peanut butter, maple syrup, vanilla extract, and almond milk. Mix well to combine.

2   Add the rolled oats, chia seeds and thoroughly stir with a spoon to combine.

3   Divide the mixture in small mason jars (or bowls), cover and refrigerate overnight.

4   Optional - Before serving, top with fresh banana slices, chopped peanuts and drizzle with peanut butter.

 CALORIES 387

CARBS 63G

 PROTEIN 11G

 FAT 11G

Nutritional Advice
Option to use honey or agave syrup instead of maple syrup. Use any type of milk for non dairy free. Use sunflower seed butter instead of nut butter for nut free.

BANANA BAKED OATMEAL

Great for a healthy make ahead for breakfast.

 10 MINS **SERVES 6**

INGREDIENTS

200g rolled oats

1 tsp cinnamon

1 tsp baking powder

¼ tsp salt

2 over ripe bananas

250ml almond milk

65g creamy peanut butter

2 tbsp maple syrup

1 tbsp ground flaxseed

1 teaspoon vanilla extract

METHOD

1 Preheat the oven to 190°C. In an 8×11 inch baking dish, combine the oats, cinnamon, baking powder and salt.

2 In a large mixing bowl, mash the bananas, then add the almond milk, peanut butter, maple syrup, flaxseed and vanilla extract. Allow the mixture to stand for 5 minutes for the flaxseed to set.

3 Pour over the wet ingredients over the oat mixture and stir to combine.

4 Bake uncovered in the preheated oven until the top of the oatmeal is golden and the mixture is set, about 30-35 minutes. Remove and allow it to cool for 5 minutes.

5 Serve with your choice of toppings

CALORIES
240

CARBS
35G

PROTEIN
7G

FAT
9G

COCOA CHIA YOGURT PUDDING

A filling, high protein breakfast or snack.

 10 MINS   **SERVES 4**

INGREDIENTS

60g chia seeds
120ml boiled hot water
3 tbsp honey
2 tsp vanilla extract
pinch of salt
375g Greek yogurt
360ml almond milk, unsweetened
3 tbsp unsweetened cocoa powder
1 tsp. ground cinnamon

Toppings
2 bananas, sliced
2 tbsp walnuts

Optional
Top with 2 tbsp cacao nibs or chocolate chips

METHOD

1   Place the chia seeds and hot water into a bowl and set aside to cool for 5 minutes.

2   Stir in the honey, vanilla extract and a pinch of salt. Now add the yogurt, almond milk, cocoa powder and cinnamon, and whisk to combine.

3   Prepare 4 glasses or jars and fill them up almost half way with the chia pudding. Next layer with sliced banana, before covering with the remaining pudding. Top the puddings with the remaining banana and walnuts.

4   Top the puddings with the remaining banana, cocoa nibs, and walnuts.

5   Set aside in the refrigerator to chill for 1 hour before serving.

These puddings can be stored in the refrigerator for 4-5 days.

CALORIES
220

CARBS
35G

PROTEIN
13G

FAT
5G

STRAWBERRY PROTEIN CHIA PUDDING

A quick and super healthy breakfast or snack.

 2 MINS **SERVES 2**

INGREDIENTS

100g frozen strawberries

100ml milk (or alternative milk for dairy free)

1 tbsp vanilla whey protein (or alternative protein powder for dairy free)

1 tbsp maple syrup

50g chia seeds

METHOD

1 Blitz the strawberries, milk, whey and maple syrup in a speed blender or food processor.

2 Add the chia seeds and mix well. Leave to thicken in the fridge for 10 minutes, mixing 2-3 times, to ensure it thickens evenly. Serve straight away or store in a refrigerator.

3 If you leave the pudding in the fridge overnight, you might want to add some extra milk to it before serving as it will become more thick as the chia seeds absorb the liquid.

CALORIES
243

CARBS
22G

PROTEIN
7G

FAT
16G

Nutritional Advice
Use a plant based protein powder for a dairy free pudding

OVERNIGHT SALTED CARAMEL OATS

Deliciously satisfying breakfast.

 10 MINS **SERVES 2**

INGREDIENTS

70g rolled oats

1 tbsp chia seeds

150ml unsweetened almond milk

¼ tsp vanilla extract

For the caramel:

1 tbsp peanut butter

1 tbsp maple syrup

pinch of salt

For the topping:

2 squares dark chocolate, melted

METHOD

1   Place the ingredients for the oat base into a bowl, stir to combine and allow to sit for a few minutes to thicken.

2   Prepare the caramel by mixing the ingredients together, then pour the caramel mixture over the oat base.

3   Finally, drizzle the melted chocolate over the caramel layer, and place in the refrigerator overnight.

CALORIES
407

CARBS
50G

PROTEIN
11G

FAT
20G

TIRAMISU OVERNIGHT WEETABIX

Ultra indulgent, sweet and healthy!

 10 MINS   **SERVES 1**

INGREDIENTS

2 weetabix

100ml black coffee

50g light cream cheese

75g plain fat free yoghurt

1/4 tsp vanilla extract

3 tbsp stevia / sweetener

1 tsp unsweetened cocoa powder

Sprinkle of cocoa powder for dusting

METHOD

1   Brew the coffee and mix in 1 tsp cocoa powder.

2   Mix the cream cheese, yoghurt, sweetener and vanilla extract and set aside.

3   Crush the weetabix into a container and pour on the coffee. Mix together.

4   Layer the tiramisu by alternating the weetabix and the cream cheese mix until there is two layers of both.

5   Refrigerate for at least 30 minutes or overnight for extra density.

6   Top with a sprinkle of cocoa powder and serve.

CALORIES
237

CARBS
41G

PROTEIN
13G

FAT
3G

OVERNIGHT WEETABIX WITH BERRIES

An easy breakfast idea which saves time in the morning!

🕐 **5 MINS**   👤 **SERVES 1**

INGREDIENTS

2 weetabix

100ml milk (almond is used for this recipe)

2 tsp honey (or maple syrup)

1/2 banana, sliced

100g greek yoghurt (or dairy free yoghurt)

METHOD

1   Crush up the 2 weetabix in a container or bowl. Add 1 tsp honey and milk, mix together and flatten the mixture to make an even layer.

2   In a separate bowl, add the yoghurt, 1 tsp honey and mix together.

3   Using the back of the spoon, level out the yoghurt on top. Then add the mixed berries on top.

4   Place the lid on and refrigerate for a few hours or overnight.

CALORIES
305

CARBS
57G

PROTEIN
14G

FAT
2G

QUINOA POWER PORRIDGE

Super healthy breakfast.

 5 MINS   **SERVES 2**

INGREDIENTS

85g dried quinoa

240ml water

240ml milk (dairy free if preferred)

2 apples, chopped

½ tsp ground cinnamon

1 tsp vanilla extract

1 tbsp ground flaxseed

METHOD

1 Rinse the quinoa under cold running water, then place in a small pot and add the water. Bring to the boil, then reduce heat, and cook for 10 minutes.

2 Now add the milk, apple, cinnamon, vanilla extract and flaxseed to the quinoa and cook for a further 5 minutes until creamy.

3 Divide the porridge between 2 bowls and serve immediately.

CALORIES
283

CARBS
54G

PROTEIN
8G

FAT
5G

Breakfast

HIGH PROTEIN

STRAWBERRY PROTEIN SMOOTHIE BOWL

A sweet, high protein treat!

 15 MINS   **SERVES 4**

INGREDIENTS

600g cottage cheese

225g frozen strawberries, thawed

4 tbsp maple syrup

225g granola

150g mixed berries

METHOD

1   Place the cottage cheese, strawberries and maple syrup in a food processor or high-speed blender and blitz until smooth and creamy.

2   Divide between 4 serving bowls, top with granola and fresh berries, to serve.

CALORIES
315

CARBS
37G

PROTEIN
19G

FAT
10G

SMOKED SALMON BREAKFAST TACOS

Start your day off in style!

 15 MINS **SERVES 4**

INGREDIENTS

8 corn tortillas

6 eggs

salt & pepper

2 tbsp chives, sliced

1 tbsp olive oil

½ red onion, diced

60g smoked salmon, torn into smaller pieces

2 tbsp feta cheese, cubed

1 lime, wedges

METHOD

1   Warm the tortillas in a dry pan over a medium heat. Remove from the pan, cover with tin foil, and keep the tortillas warm until ready to serve.

2   In a small bowl, whisk the eggs, season to taste with salt and pepper and mix in the chives.

3   Heat the olive oil in a pan over a medium heat and cook the onion for 2-3 minutes. Add in the eggs and cook, stirring often. When eggs are still slightly runny, add the smoked salmon and cubed feta. Continue cooking until the eggs are no longer runny.

4   Divide the scrambled eggs evenly between the warm tortillas, then top with additional chives. Serve immediately with a wedge of lime.

CALORIES
313

CARBS
30G

PROTEIN
15G

FAT
13G

Breakfast

HIGH PROTEIN

BLT EGGLETS

Tasty bacon & eggs treats.

 25 MINS   **SERVES 6**   GF

INGREDIENTS

6 eggs

2 slices smoked bacon, cut into quarters

4 tbsp mayonnaise

1 tbsp chives, chopped

1 tsp hot sauce, of choice (optional)

1 tsp red wine vinegar

salt

freshly ground black pepper

75g cherry tomatoes, quartered

1 handful Romaine lettuce, shredded

METHOD

1 Place eggs in a saucepan and cover with water. Bring the water to the boil then hard boil the eggs for 10 minutes.

2 Meanwhile, heat a large non-stick pan over medium heat, add the bacon and cook for around 6 minutes, stirring occasionally until crisp. Remove from the heat and transfer the bacon to a plate line with kitchen paper.

3 In a medium bowl, whisk together the mayonnaise, chives, hot sauce and vinegar, and season with salt and pepper.

4 Peel and halve the eggs. Spread the mayonnaise mixture on the cut side of one egg half. Top with tomatoes, lettuce, and bacon; then top with another egg half. Continue this process with the remaining eggs. Season with salt and black pepper and serve.

CALORIES
174

CARBS
1G

PROTEIN
8G

FAT
15G

AIR FRYER TURKEY BREAKFAST SAUSAGES

Tasty, impressive low calorie breakfast.

 5 MINS   SERVES 4

INGREDIENTS

450g lean turkey mince

1 tbsp coconut sugar (or white sugar)

2 tsp fresh sage leaves, finely chopped

¾ tsp salt

¾ tsp smoked paprika

½ tsp red pepper flakes

½ tsp fennel seeds, crushed

½ tsp garlic powder

olive oil cooking spray

METHOD

1   In a medium bowl, combine the turkey, sugar, sage, salt, paprika, red pepper flakes, fennel seeds, and garlic powder until evenly combined.

2   Using damp hands, form the turkey mixture into 8 thin patties about 3" (7.5cm) in diameter and ¼ " (0.5cm) thick.

3   Grease an air-fryer basket with cooking spray. Working in batches, arrange the patties in the basket, spacing about ¼" (0.5cm) apart.

4   Cook at 200°C for 5-8 minutes, flipping the patties halfway through, until golden and crisp. Continue cooking the patties until all the mixture has been used up

CALORIES
184

CARBS
4G

PROTEIN
21G

FAT
10G

HIGH PROTEIN

RED PESTO, AVOCADO & SOFT EGG TOAST

A super quick breakfast, high in protein and good fats,

 6 MINS **SERVES 2**

INGREDIENTS

4 eggs
2 slices wholegrain bread, toasted
4 tbsp red pesto
1 avocado, sliced

METHOD

1. Bring a small pot of water to a boil. Add the eggs, cover and continue to boil for six minutes (or longer, depending on how you like your eggs cooked).

2. After six minutes, remove the eggs from the pot and run them under cold water until they are cool enough to handle and peel.

3. Toast the bread and spread each slice with 2 tablespoons of the red pesto, then top with the sliced avocado and eggs.

CALORIES
479

CARBS
29G

PROTEIN
22G

FAT
32G

Nutritional Advice
The bread you use may alter the calories and nutrition slightly.

TOMATO AND EGG BREAKFAST PIZZA

Breakfast packed full of flavour!

 10 MINS **SERVES 2**

INGREDIENTS

4 eggs

salt & pepper

½ red onion, chopped

1 tbsp olive oil

1 large tomato, sliced

1 tbsp dried oregano

40g ham, chopped

55g grated cheddar cheese

METHOD

1   Whisk the eggs in a bowl, season with salt and pepper, and stir through the red onion.

2   Heat the olive oil in a non-stick frying pan over a medium heat. Place a layer of tomatoes in the bottom of the pan and cook for 2-3 minutes.

3   Pour the eggs over the tomatoes, sprinkle with half the oregano and cook for 2-3 minutes.

4   Now scatter over the ham and cheese and add the remaining oregano. Cook for a further 2-3 minutes until the eggs are set. Slice and serve immediately.

CALORIES
308

CARBS
5G

PROTEIN
21G

FAT
23G

PROTEIN ORANGE & YOGHURT PANCAKES

Tasty, impressive low calorie breakfast.

 5 MINS   **SERVES 2**

INGREDIENTS

2 tsp orange peel

orange slices, to serve

2 eggs

160g soy yoghurt
(or natural yoghurt if
preferred)

2 tsp sugar

2 tsp vanilla extract

120g wholemeal flour (or
all purpose if preferred)

1 tsp baking powder

1 tsp coconut oil, melted

METHOD

1 Mix the egg, yogurt, sugar, vanilla extract and
orange peel. Fold in the flour and baking powder
and mix well until smooth. Lastly, add in the
melted coconut oil and mix again.

2 Fry the pancakes on a dry non-stick pan over low-
medium heat until golden brown.

3 Serve with slices of orange and fresh berries.

CALORIES
259

CARBS
48G

PROTEIN
18G

FAT
12G

LEMON PANCAKES

A quick, delicious breakfast or sweet snack.

 10 MINS SERVES 2

INGREDIENTS

For the pancakes:

65g oat flour (or approx 50g all purpose flour if preferred)

1½ tsp baking powder

1 tsp honey

120ml oat milk

1 egg

1 tsp lemon zest

1 tbsp coconut oil (or olive oil if preferred)

Toppings:

4 tbsp greek yoghurt

2 lemon slices

1 tsp lemon juice

1 tsp lemon zest

2 tbsp honey

METHOD

1   Place all the pancake ingredients (except for the oil) into a large bowl and mix to form a batter.

2   Place a non-stick pan over medium-high heat and warm up some coconut oil. Scoop about ¼ cup of the pancake batter into the pan and cook until bubbles appear on the surface. Flip the pancake over and cook for another minute, then remove from the pan.

3   Repeat this process with the remaining pancake batter.

4   Serve the pancakes topped with greek yoghurt, a slice of lemon, a little lemon zest and juice, and some honey.

CALORIES
293

CARBS
31G

PROTEIN
12G

FAT
14G

LOW
CALORIE

VANILLA PROTEIN PANCAKES

Super simple, high protein snack.

 10 MINS   **SERVES 10**

INGREDIENTS

2 eggs

300ml almond milk, unsweetened

130g self raising flour

60g plant-based vanilla protein powder

Oil for frying

To serve

160g fresh or frozen berries to serve

4 tbsp honey to drizzle

METHOD

1   In a large bowl, mix together the eggs and almond milk

2   Next, add in the flour and protein powder, and mix until well combined.

3   Heat the oil in a frying pan

4   Pour scoops of the batter into your frying pan and cook the pancakes accordingly. This mixture provides 10 large scoops.

5   Remove the pancakes and set aside, then repeat the process to use up the remaining batter.

6   Serve with fresh or frozen berries and drizzles of honey.

CALORIES
106

CARBS
16G

PROTEIN
7G

FAT
1G

PROTEIN WAFFLES / PANCAKES

Healthy protein waffles.

 10 MINS **SERVES 4**

INGREDIENTS

2 eggs

300ml almond milk, unsweetened

1 tsp vanilla extract

130g whole wheat flour (or all-purpose flour)

60g plant-based vanilla protein powder

½ tsp baking powder

½ tsp baking soda

2 tbsp melted coconut oil, or alternative oil if preferred

To serve

160g berries to serve

4 tbsp maple syrup or honey to drizzle

METHOD

1 Heat up the waffle maker for the waffles

2 In a large bowl, mix together the eggs, almond milk, and vanilla extract.

3 Next, add in the flour, protein powder, baking powder, baking soda, and mix until well combined.

4 **Waffles**
Now, add in the oil and mix again. Pour a portion of the batter into your waffle maker and cook accordingly

Pancakes
Heat the oil in a pan and pour a portion of the batter into your pan and cook until golden brown

5 Remove the waffles / pancakes and set aside, then repeat the process to use up the remaining batter.

6 Serve with fresh berries and a drizzle of maple syrup or honey.

CALORIES
336

CARBS
41G

PROTEIN
17G

FAT
11G

Breakfast

Lunch

TURKEY BURGERS

Low calorie and super simple. Delicious filling lunch or dinner.

 10 MINS  **SERVES 4**

INGREDIENTS

500g lean turkey mince
2 tsp italian seasoning
2 tsp smoked paprika
1 tsp onion powder
1/2 tsp garlic powder
1/4 tsp salt
1/4 tsp pepper

METHOD

1   Add all ingredients to a bowl and mix well with hands

2   Roll into 4 balls and flatten each ball to make a burger patty

3   Fry on a medium heat for 5 minutes each side

4   Serve in a burger bun, with salad, or store in the fridge for the next day

CALORIES
148

CARBS
1G

PROTEIN
31G

FAT
2G

HIGH PROTEIN

CHEESY CHICKEN TINGA QUASEDILLAS

A tasty lunch which uses the slow cooker Chicken Tinga.

 15 MINS   **SERVES 4**

INGREDIENTS

For avocado salsa:
1 tomato
½ white onion
1 garlic clove
1 jalapeño pepper
10 sprigs coriander
1 avocado
salt & pepper

For the wraps:
4 flour tortilla wraps
4 servings Slow-Cooker Chicken Tinga (see recipe pg 94)
8 tbsp grated cheddar cheese

METHOD

1   Place all the avocado salsa ingredients into a food processor, season with salt and pepper and blitz until combined. Set aside until needed.

2   Heat a tortilla wrap in a frying pan over a medium heat. Cover half of the flour tortilla with a serving of the slow cooker chicken tinga and 2 tablespoons of grated cheese.

3   Fold the wrap over onto itself, and cook each side over a medium-high heat for 3-4 minutes, until crispy and starting to brown.

4   Remove from the pan and repeat this process with the remaining tortillas. Once cooked, cut each wrap in half and serve immediately with the avocado salsa.

CALORIES
529

CARBS
37G

PROTEIN
45G

FAT
22G

TURKEY & SWEET POTATO SLIDERS

A super healthy alternative for your lunch!

 8 MINS SERVES 4 DF GF

INGREDIENTS

3 sweet potatoes, sliced
into ½ inch (1.25cm)
rounds

3 tbsp olive oil

For the turkey sliders:

450g lean turkey mince

2 tbsp spring onion, sliced

1 egg

55g almond flour (or
regular flour)

½ tsp paprika

1 tbsp yeast

1 tbsp tamari

1 tsp Dijon mustard

salt & pepper to taste

METHOD

1   Preheat the oven to 180°C. Line a baking sheet
    with baking paper.

2   Lay the sliced sweet potatoes on the baking sheet,
    drizzle with 1 tablespoon of olive oil and season
    with salt and pepper. Place the baking sheet into
    the oven and bake the sweet potatoes for 20
    minutes.

3   Place all the ingredients for the turkey sliders into
    a large bowl and mix to combine. Using your hands
    shape the mixture into 8 even-sized patties.

4   Heat the remaining 2 tablespoons of olive oil in a
    skillet over a medium heat. Cook the patties for
    about 3 minutes on each side, until browned and
    cooked through.

5   To assemble the sliders, sandwich the turkey patty
    in between two sweet potato slices, adding the
    toppings of your choice. Serve immediately.

CALORIES
424

CARBS
24G

PROTEIN
29G

FAT
25G

Nutritional Advice
Regular flour can be used
as an alternative at
the ratio 1:1

Lunch

HIGH PROTEIN

SHAKSHUKA

A very tasty, high protein lunch, easy to make.

 20 MINS **SERVES 2**

INGREDIENTS

1 white onion, sliced

2 bell peppers, sliced

2x 400g cans chopped tomatoes

4 eggs

15g parsley leaves, chopped

1 tbsp olive oil

Salt & pepper

METHOD

1   Heat the oil a large non-stick frying pan over a medium-high heat. Add the onion and bell peppers, stirring constantly, and cook, for 5 minutes or until the onion and pepper have softened.

2   Add the chopped tomatoes and cook, stirring for a further 5 minutes.

3   Use a spoon to make 4 large holes in the tomato mixture, then crack an egg into each hole. Reduce the heat to low, and partially cover the pan with a lid. Cook for 10 minutes or until eggs are cooked to your liking. Sprinkle with parsley and serve immediately.

CALORIES
308

CARBS
22G

PROTEIN
16G

FAT
17G

COTTAGE CHEESE PROTEIN OMELETTE

A quick tasty, high protein healthy lunch.

 10 MINS **SERVES 1**

INGREDIENTS

2 large eggs, beaten

¼ tsp salt, divided

¼ tsp black pepper, divided

70g cottage cheese

1 tsp Italian herbs

2 tsp butter

30g baby spinach

1 small garlic clove, peeled & crushed

2 tsp olive oil

2 tbsp Parmesan cheese, freshly grated

1 spring onion, sliced

METHOD

1   Crack the eggs into a small bowl, beat until well combined and season with a pinch of salt and pepper. Set aside.

2   In another bowl, combine the cottage cheese with the Italian herbs and remaining salt & pepper. Set aside.

3   Heat a non-stick pan over medium heat and add the butter. Once the butter is hot, add the spinach and garlic. Stir-fry the spinach for 1-2 minutes until it wilts. Then remove from the pan and set aside.

4   Return the pan to medium heat and add the olive oil. Reduce the heat to medium-low and pour in the beaten eggs, tilting the pan to ensure the egg mixture spreads evenly across the base.

5   As the edges of the omelette start to set, gently lift them with a spatula to allow the uncooked eggs from the middle to run underneath and cook.

6   Once the centre of the omelette starts to set, sprinkle the freshly grated Parmesan cheese, then top with the cooked spinach and the seasoned cottage cheese mixture.

7   Fold the omelette in half, reduce the heat to low, and continue cooking for a few minutes.

8   Gently slide the omelette onto a plate, top with the sliced green onions and serve.

CALORIES
430

CARBS
6G

PROTEIN
26G

FAT
34G

HIGH
PROTEIN

BAKED FETA PASTA

A superior, tasty dish for the family to enjoy.

 5 MINS SERVES 4

INGREDIENTS

300g cherry tomatoes

2 shallots, sliced

2 cloves garlic, crushed

2 tbsp olive oil, divided

salt

1 pinch of crushed red pepper flakes

225g feta cheese

3 sprigs fresh thyme

280g pasta of choice

zest of 1 lemon

4 tbsp fresh basil, for garnish

METHOD

1 Preheat the oven to 200°C.

2 In a medium baking dish, add the tomatoes, shallots, garlic, and 1 tablespoon of olive oil. Season with salt and red pepper flakes and toss to combine.

3 Place the feta cheese into the centre and drizzle with the remaining 1 tablespoon of olive oil. Scatter the thyme over the tomatoes.

4 Place the dish into the oven to bake for 40-45 minutes, until the tomatoes start to burst and the feta cheese is golden on top.

5 Meanwhile, cook the pasta to al dente, according to package directions.

6 Add the cooked pasta and lemon zest to the feta cheese and tomatoes and stir until combined. Garnish with basil and serve immediately.

CALORIES
435

CARBS
48G

PROTEIN
12G

FAT
20G

HIGH PROTEIN

MEXICAN BOWL

Nutritious, high protein bowl of Mexican goodness.

🕐 **15 MINS**   👤 **SERVES 4**   GF

INGREDIENTS

1 sweet potato, cubed

2 tbsp olive oil

salt & pepper,

pinch chilli powder

2 servings Turkey Chorizo (see recipe on pg 42)

400g can black beans, drained

1 tsp ground cumin

4 eggs

1 avocado, sliced

Topping

4 tbsp coriander, chopped

4 tbsp greek yoghurt

METHOD

1   Heat oven to 200°C.

2   Place the sweet potato onto a baking sheet, drizzle with olive oil, season with a generous pinch of salt, pepper and chilli powder, and toss to combine. Place the baking sheet into the hot oven and roast the sweet potato for around 20 minutes, until cooked.

3   While the sweet potato is cooking, make the Turkey Chorizo (see recipe on pg 42).

4   Place the black beans into a small pan, season with salt, pepper and ground cumin, then heat up gently over medium heat.

5   Fry the eggs to your liking.

6   Once the sweet potatoes are cooked, divide equally between 4 bowls. Top with the turkey chorizo, black beans and avocado.

7   Then top with the fried egg, and garnish with coriander and a spoon of yogurt.

CALORIES
454

CARBS
30G

PROTEIN
26G

FAT
27G

Lunch

SMASHED PITTA BURGER WITH TZAZIKI

A tasty, wholesome dinner with a fresh tzakiki dip.

 10 MINS   SERVES 4

INGREDIENTS

For the tzatziki:
½ cucumber, grated
190g Greek yogurt
juice from 1 lemon
1 clove garlic, minced
2 tbsp fresh dill, chopped
2 tbsp fresh mint, chopped
1 tbsp olive oil
1 tsp salt

For the burger:
450g minced lamb
½ red onion, grated
3 cloves garlic, minced
2 tbsp fresh mint
½ tsp dried oregano
½ tsp paprika
1 tsp salt
½ tsp black pepper
4x pitta bread

Toppings:
1 cucumber, chopped, garnish
150g cherry tomatoes
4 tbsp feta cheese, crumbled
fresh dill, chopped
fresh mint, chopped

METHOD

1   To make the tzatziki, grate the cucumber. Place the cucumber onto some kitchen towel, and squeeze out any excess liquid from the cucumber.

2   In a medium bowl, combine the grated cucumber, yogurt, lemon juice, garlic, dill, mint, olive oil and salt. Refrigerate until ready to serve.

3   Place the lamb into a large bowl, adding the onion, garlic, mint, oregano, paprika, salt and black pepper. Mix until fully combined, then roll into 4 even-sized balls.

4   Heat a cast iron skillet / pan over medium-high heat. Place the balls of meat on the hot surface then, using a heavy pan or burger press, smash the pitta bread down on top of the burger until it's as flat as you can make it.

5   Cook for 4-5 minutes until the meat is cooked through, then flip over and cook for a further minute.

6   Remove from the skillet / pan and serve the burger with tzatziki and other toppings

CALORIES
569

CARBS
42G

PROTEIN
30G

FAT
32G

Lunch

TURKEY CHORIZO

A quick, tasty lunch, perfect in the Mexican bowl!

⏱ **5 MINS**   👤 **SERVES 4**   *DF* *GF*

INGREDIENTS

1 tbsp. olive oil
450g lean turkey mince
¾ -1 tsp salt
2 tsp chilli powder
2 tsp smoked paprika
1 tsp ground cumin
1 tsp ground coriander
1 tsp garlic powder
¼ tsp red pepper flakes
1 tbsp red wine vinegar

METHOD

1   Heat the olive oil in a large frying pan over medium heat. Add the remaining ingredients to the pan, mixing to combine and breaking up the turkey.

2   Cook the mixture for 10 minutes, until the turkey is browned and cooked through. Remove from the heat and place in a bowl, or set aside in the refrigerator until you are ready to use.

3   Use as part of the Mexican Breakfast Bowl recipe!

CALORIES
213

CARBS
2G

PROTEIN
22G

FAT
13G

HIGH PROTEIN

TANDOORI BOWL

A tasty, quick high protein meal.

 10 MINS   **SERVES 2**

INGREDIENTS

½ head cauliflower, cut into florets

100g chickpeas, drained

300g boneless, skinless, chicken breast

1 red onion, sliced in wedges

2 tbsp olive oil

¾ tsp salt

½ tsp black pepper

2 tbsp garam masala spice

240g cooked white basmati rice

2 servings, Coriander & Mint Dip (see recipe on pg 114)

METHOD

1   Preheat the oven to 220°C. Line a baking sheet with baking paper.

2   Place the cauliflower, chickpeas, chicken and onion on the baking sheet and drizzle with olive oil. Season with salt, pepper and garam masala spice, and stir to combine.

3   Place the baking sheet in the oven and cook for 25 minutes, removing halfway through to give the ingredients a quick mix.

4   Serve over rice with the Coriander & Mint Dip.

CALORIES
653

CARBS
71G

PROTEIN
47G

FAT
21G

Lunch

TUNA MELT STUFFED PEPPERS

A quick tasty, healthy lunch for the family.

 10 MINS   **SERVES 2**

INGREDIENTS

1 red bell pepper, cut in half & seeds removed

1 tbsp olive oil

140g can tuna, drained

1 celery stalk, diced

4 tbsp shredded carrots

2 tbsp chopped spring onion

2 tbsp plain greek yogurt

1 tsp dijon mustard

salt & pepper, to taste

4 tbsp grated cheddar cheese

1 tbsp coriander, chopped - to garnish

sliced spring onion for garnish

METHOD

1   Preheat the oven to 200°C. Line a baking sheet with baking paper.

2   Add bell peppers to the baking sheet and drizzle with the olive oil. Rub the outsides and insides of peppers with the oil and place into the oven to bake for 10-15 minutes until just fork tender.

3   While the peppers are baking, make the tuna mixture. Add the drained tuna, celery, carrots, spring onion, Greek yogurt, hot sauce and Dijon mustard to a bowl, then season to taste with salt and pepper.

4   Evenly divide the tuna mixture into each of the cooked bell pepper halves. Sprinkle the cheddar cheese on top, and place the sheet back into the oven to bake for a further 5 minutes, until the cheese has melted.

5   Garnish with coriander and spring onion and serve.

CALORIES
321

CARBS
10G

PROTEIN
26G

FAT
20G

HIGH
PROTEIN

ASIAN CHICKEN LETTUCE WRAPS

A quick, tasty, high protein lunch or dinner.

 20 MINS **SERVES 5**

INGREDIENTS

For the sauce:

4 tbsp tamari

3 tbsp smooth peanut butter

3 tbsp honey

1 tbsp rice vinegar

2 tbsp olive oil

1 tsp sriracha

¼ tsp paprika

¼ tsp garlic powder

To serve:

400g cooked shredded chicken breast

1 red bell pepper, diced

1 head romaine lettuce

50g peanuts

2 spring onions

METHOD

1 Place all the sauce ingredients into a large bowl and whisk until well combined. Add the shredded chicken and diced bell pepper and toss to coat in the sauce.

2 Serve the chicken mixture in a lettuce wrap, and top with peanuts and green onions.

CALORIES
357

CARBS
21G

PROTEIN
32G

FAT
18G

Lunch

HIGH PROTEIN

TACO TOMATOES

High protein, low carb lunch.

 5 MINS **SERVES 4**

INGREDIENTS

1 tbsp olive oil

1 medium white onion, chopped

450g 5% fat minced beef

1x 28g packet taco seasoning

4 large, ripe beefsteak tomatoes

50g cheddar cheese, grated

4 tbsp sour cream

METHOD

1 Heat the olive oil in a large frying pan over a medium heat, add the onion and cook, stirring often, for 5 minutes until soft.

2 Add the beef and taco seasoning and continue to cook for 8 minutes, breaking up the meat with a wooden spoon, until no longer pink.

3 Place the tomatoes on a board, stem-side down, and slice into 6 wedges, taking care not to cut the tomatoes all the way through. Carefully spread open the wedges.

4 Divide the taco meat evenly between the 4 tomatoes, then top each with cheddar cheese and sour cream before serving.

CALORIES
357

CARBS
13G

PROTEIN
28G

FAT
22G

COURGETTE & SWEETCORN FRITTERS

A filling healthy snack with 4 fritters per serving.

 5 MINS SERVES 3

INGREDIENTS

2 medium courgettes

160g canned sweetcorn

25g parmesan cheese, grated

1 small onion, grated

1 clove garlic, minced

1 tbsp dried parsley

1 tbsp dried parsley

½ tsp dried oregano

1 tsp salt

½ tsp freshly ground black pepper

½ tsp freshly ground black pepper

2 eggs, beaten

120g all-purpose flour

1 tsp baking powder

METHOD

1   Shred the courgette using the large holes on the grater and transfer onto a kitchen towel.

2   Wrap the towel around the courgette and squeeze out as much moisture as possible.

3   Heat the oil in a pan over medium heat. Add the onion and cook for 3 minutes until softened and browned.

4   Now place the courgette into a large bowl. Add the sweetcorn, parmesan, onion, garlic, parsley, basil, oregano, salt, pepper, paprika and beaten eggs to the bowl, and stir to combine.

5   Now add the flour and baking powder to the mixture, and stir until well combined. If the mixture is too wet, add a little more flour. The drier the courgette, the less flour you'll need to use.

6   Shape the mixture into 12 even sized patties.

7   Place the patties onto a tray and place the tray into the freezer for around 5 to 8 minutes to firm the patties up a little.

8   In the meantime, preheat the Air Fryer to 180°C.

Or preheat oven to 220°C.

9   **Air fryer**: Working in batches, place the patties in the air fryer basket in a single layer and cook for 6 minutes, then flip over and continue cooking for a further 6-8 minutes, until golden.

Oven: Place the patties in the oven on a lined baking tray and cook for 20 minutes, or until golden.

10 Continue cooking the fritters until all the batter has been used up.

CALORIES
312

CARBS
52G

PROTEIN
13G

FAT
7G

CHICKEN TINGA BOWL

Tasty lunch which makes great use of the slow cooked Chicken Tinga.

 10 MINS **SERVES 4**

INGREDIENTS

1 red bell pepper, sliced

1 yellow bell pepper, sliced

2 tbsp olive oil

salt & pepper

4 servings Slow-Cooker Chicken Tinga (see recipe pg 94)

400g cooked quinoa

400g can black beans

4 tbsp coriander, chopped

1 lime, wedges

METHOD

1   Preheat the oven to 220°C.

2   Arrange the bell peppers on a baking sheet, toss with olive oil and season with salt and pepper. Place in the hot oven to roast for 30 minutes.

3   In the meantime, heat up the slow cooked chicken tinga and cook your quinoa.

4   Serve the chicken with the roasted peppers, quinoa, and black beans. Garnish with cilantro and serve with lime wedges.

CALORIES
545

CARBS
57G

PROTEIN
47G

FAT
10G

MEXICAN STUFFED PEPPERS

Simple, low calorie recipe using just 5 ingredients.

 10 MINS   SERVES 4

INGREDIENTS

4 bell peppers

400g 5% fat beef mince

400g can chopped tomatoes

160g cooked rice

2 tbsp Mexican spice blend / seasoning

METHOD

1   Preheat the oven to 190°C. Heat a large pan over a medium-high heat and cook the beef for 5-7 minutes until browned.

2   Add in the tomatoes and rice and bring to the boil, then reduce the heat and simmer gently, covered, for around 6-8 minutes.

3   Meanwhile, cut off the tops from peppers and remove the seeds from the inside. Place the peppers on a baking dish and fill the peppers with the beef mixture.

4   Cover the dish with kitchen foil and bake in the oven for 35 minutes, or until the peppers are tender. Remove from oven and serve.

CALORIES
281

CARBS
23G

PROTEIN
23G

FAT
10G

Nutritional Advice
Check seasoning for gluten.

DETOX SALAD

A bowl full of goodness which will see you through the rest of the day!

 10 MINS   **SERVES 2**

INGREDIENTS

1 avocado, peeled, stone removed, cut into cubes

2 bunches parsley, roughly chopped, around 30g

46g cooked quinoa

½ cucumber, cut into cubes

½ courgette, cut into cubes

1 small red onion, finely diced

1 tsp olive oil

juice of 1 lemon

30g mixed seeds and nuts, to garnish

METHOD

1 In a medium bowl, add parsley, avocado, quinoa, cucumber, courgette, and onion and toss to combine.

2 Drizzle with olive oil and lemon, season with salt and pepper, then mix to combine and serve sprinkled with nuts and seeds.

CALORIES
315

CARBS
19G

PROTEIN
10G

FAT
24G

LOW CALORIE

PESTO WHITE FISH

A tasty quick & easy healthy lunch.

 5 MINS SERVES 2

INGREDIENTS

2x 170g white fish fillets of choice (e.g. cod)

1 tbsp olive oil

salt to taste

½ onion, sliced

2 tbsp pesto

8 cherry tomatoes, halved

2 slices lemon

METHOD

1. Preheat the oven to 200°C. Prepare 2 large pieces of parchment paper, big enough to hold the fish and fold over.

2. Rub the fish fillets with olive oil, and season with salt.

3. Layer the sliced onion in the centre of each piece of parchment paper, then place the fish fillets on top. Brush the fish with pesto and then top with the cherry tomatoes, finally topping with the sliced lemon.

4. Fold the parchment paper over the fillet and pinch the edges to seal the parcel tight.

5. Place the parcels on a baking sheet, in the oven, and bake for 15 minutes.

6. Once ready, remove from the oven and allow to cool slightly. Open the parchment paper carefully to release the hot steam, taking care not to burn yourself.

CALORIES
190

CARBS
8G

PROTEIN
21G

FAT
7G

Lunch

PINEAPPLE PRAWN RICE

A super yummy, low fat, high protein meal.

 5 MINS SERVES 4

INGREDIENTS

185g uncooked Jasmine rice

1 tsp coconut oil (or olive oil if preferred)

680g jumbo prawn, peeled

salt & black pepper

1 red bell pepper, chopped (or use a mix of colours)

For the sauce:

400g can pineapple, reserve all liquid

juice from 1 orange

2 tbsp tomato ketchup

1 tbsp fresh ginger

2 tbsp tamari sauce

1½ tbsp cornstarch + 1 tbsp. water, mixed

To garnish:

4 tbsp coriander, chopped

1 tbsp sesame seeds

METHOD

1 Cook the rice according to instructions on the packaging.

2 Transfer all of the liquid from the canned pineapple into a mixing bowl, place the pineapple aside. Add the remaining ingredients for the sauce into the pineapple juice and mix well.

3 Heat the oil in a large wok over medium-high heat, and add the prawns. Season with salt & pepper and cook for 2-3 minutes. Add the bell pepper and cook for a further 2 minutes.

4 Reduce the heat to medium and pour in the sauce, then add in the cornstarch mixture and stir immediately.

5 Stir in the cooked rice and serve with a garnish of coriander and sesame seeds.

CALORIES
382

CARBS
51G

PROTEIN
39G

FAT
3G

Nutritional Advice
Check seasoning for gluten.

Lunch

VEGETABLE CHILLI SALAD

Only 5 ingredients for this healthy filling lunch, no cooking involved!

 10 MINS SERVES 4

INGREDIENTS

1 x 400g can black beans, rinsed, drained

1 x 200g can sweet corn, rinsed, drained

1 red bell pepper, sliced

bunch coriander, chopped

150g hot salsa

METHOD

1   Rinse the black beans and corn under cold running water, rinse thoroughly and drain well. Slice the pepper into small strips. Chop the coriander coarsely.

2   Mix the beans, corn, pepper and coriander with the salsa in a medium bowl. This salad can be stored in an airtight container in the refrigerator for up to 3 days.

CALORIES
144

CARBS
28G

PROTEIN
8G

FAT
2G

HIGH PROTEIN

TUNA & TOMATO SALAD

High protein, light lunch.

 10 MINS SERVES 4

INGREDIENTS

5 large tomatoes,
chopped into chunks

1 white onion, sliced

400g drained tuna, flakes

80g olives

2 tbsp. olive oil

Optional:

1 tsp paprika

salt & pepper

METHOD

1   Place all the ingredients into a large serving bowl.
    Drizzle over the olive oil and if preferred, season
    with salt, pepper and paprika and mix well. Serve
    immediately.

CALORIES
219

CARBS
8G

PROTEIN
26G

FAT
10G

ASPARAGUS & LEEK QUICHE

Tasty and nutritious, full of fresh ingredients and ideal for a lunch or dinner.

 10 MINS   **SERVES 6**

INGREDIENTS

1 tbsp butter

140g asparagus spears, trimmed & cut into ½ inch pieces

1 leek, (white & light green parts only), thinly sliced

salt & pepper

3 eggs

140g Greek yogurt

240ml milk

115g grated cheddar cheese

320g shortcrust pastry

METHOD

1   Preheat the oven to 180°C.

2   Melt the butter in a pot over a medium heat. Add the asparagus and leek, and sauté for 6-8 minutes, stirring occasionally. Season to taste with salt and pepper.

3   In a medium bowl, whisk together the eggs, Greek yogurt and milk. Season with salt and pepper.

4   Place the shortcrust pastry on a baking sheet. Sprinkle the grated cheese over the crust and top with the asparagus and leek. Now pour over the egg mixture.

5   Place the baking sheet into the hot oven and bake the quiche until the edges are set but the eggs still wobble a little in the centre. This will take roughly 35-45 minutes.

6   Once baked, set the quiche aside to cool on a wire rack for 15 minutes before slicing and serving.

7   Quiche can be served warm at room temperature, or chilled in the refrigerator and served cold.

8   Store in an airtight container in the refrigerator for 3-4 days, or in the freezer for up to 3 months.

CALORIES
430

CARBS
28G

PROTEIN
15G

FAT
28G

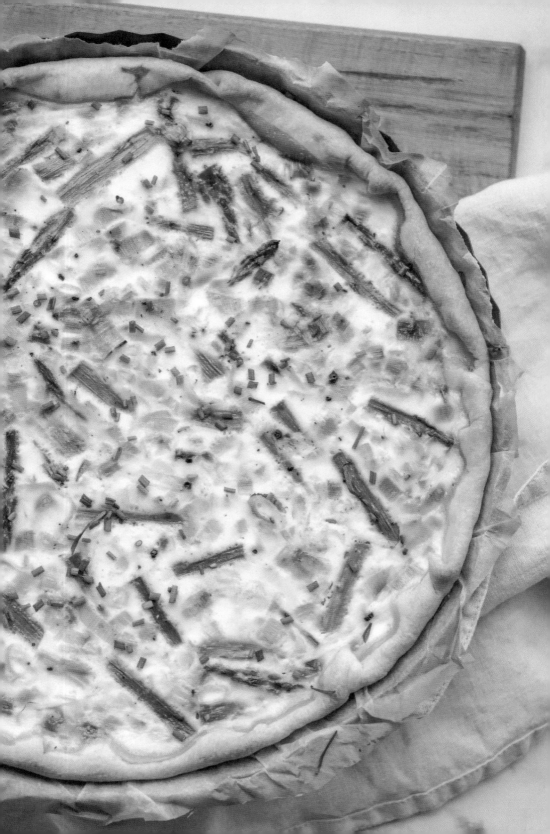

SLOW COOKER CHICKEN SOUP

Save time later with this low calorie lunch!

 5 MINS SERVES 8

INGREDIENTS

2 tbsp butter
1 onion, chopped
2 carrots, chopped
2 stalks celery, chopped
1 tsp salt
1 tsp black pepper
1 tsp dried thyme
1 tsp dried oregano
1 tbsp fresh parsley chopped
1 chicken bouillon cube
950ml chicken broth
900g chicken thighs, skinless, boneless
950ml water
100g white basmati rice

To serve:
lemon, wedges
2 tbsp parsley, chopped
2 tbsp spring onions, sliced

METHOD

1   Add the chicken broth, chicken thighs, water and rice into the slow cooker and set on high.

2   In a pan, sauté the butter, onion, carrots and celery until translucent. Season with salt and pepper, add the thyme, oregano, parsley, and chicken cube and stir. Add into the slow cooker and close the lid.

3   Add into the slow cooker, close the lid and leave to cook for a minimum of 1 hour.

4   Ensure the chicken is cooked through, and then remove and shred with two forks, then add back to the slow cooker and mix together.

5   Serve the soup with lemon wedges, and a garnish of parsley and spring onions.

CALORIES
230

CARBS
14G

PROTEIN
24G

FAT
8G

CREAMY PUMPKIN SOUP

Dairy free, healthy and easy to make!

 25 MINS SERVES 4

INGREDIENTS

2 tbsp olive oil

1 onion, chopped

3 cloves garlic, minced

900ml vegetable stock (or chicken stock)

1 can coconut milk

1 small pumpkin (approx 1.5kg) peeled and chopped into 2cm chunks

1/2 tsp ground nutmeg

Optional:

1 tsp ground coriander

1 tsp ground cumin

salt and pepper as desired

*If you struggle to peel and chop the pumpkin, place in the oven for 15 mins to soften the skin first. Allow to cool before chopping.

METHOD

1   In a large saucepan, add the oil, then sautee the onions and garlic over a low heat until they become fragrant.

2   Add the pumpkin pieces and stir well to combine with the onion and garlic. Cook for approx 5 minutes until the pumpkin starts to soften slightly.

3   Add the spices and stir well.

4   Pour in the broth. Bring the mixture to the boil, then reduce the heat to low and let it simmer for 20 - 25 mins, until the pumpkin is soft.

5   Remove from the heat. Use an immersion blender to puree the soup until smooth. For a regular blender, allow the soup to cool, then blend in batches until creamy.

6   Return the put to a low heat and stir in the coconut milk.. Let the soup simmer for another 5 minutes.

7   Season with salt and pepper and serve.

CALORIES
243

CARBS
28G

PROTEIN
4G

FAT
13G

SLOW COOKER CREAMY CHICKEN & POTATO SOUP

HIGH PROTEIN

A time saving lunch or dinner.

 5 MINS   SERVES 6

INGREDIENTS

680g boneless, skinless chicken breasts

salt & pepper

450g baby potatoes, quartered

225g cream cheese

1 white onion, chopped

1 carrot, chopped

1 jalapeño, finely chopped (optional)

4 cloves garlic, finely chopped

1 bunch thyme

960ml chicken broth

240ml whole milk

1 chicken bouillon / stock cube

2 tsp curry powder

1 tsp dried oregano

200g kale, stems removed, chopped

METHOD

1 Season the chicken with salt and pepper and place in the bottom of the slow cooker. Add the potatoes, cream cheese, onion, carrot, jalapeño, garlic, and thyme and stir to combine.

2 Now add in the chicken broth, milk, bouillon cube, curry powder, oregano and season with a little more salt and pepper.

3 Cover the slow cooked with the lid and cook on LOW for 6 hours.

4 Transfer the cooked chicken to a plate and shred the chicken using 2 forks. Return chicken to the slow cooker and add in the kale. Stir until well combined and continue to cook on low for around 10 minutes until the kale has wilted.

5 Check the soup for seasoning and add a little more salt and pepper if required, and serve.

CALORIES
367

CARBS
22G

PROTEIN
33G

FAT
16G

Nutritional Advice
Check broth / bouillon / stock cube for gluten.

Dinner

SENEGAL CHICKEN

A deliciously fresh family dinner.

 30 MINS SERVES 4

INGREDIENTS

For the chicken:

800g chicken legs, bone in & skin on

1 tsp sea salt

1 tbsp olive oil

For the marinade:

1 onion, chopped

4 garlic cloves, peeled

handful of fresh parsley

1 tsp cayenne pepper

zest & juice of 1 lemon

2 tsp dijon mustard

For the sauce:

2 tbsp olive oil

3 onions, sliced

1 red bell pepper, sliced

2 garlic cloves, minced

juice 2 lemons

2 tbsp dijon mustard

300ml chicken broth

6 sprigs fresh thyme

1 bay leaf

1 tsp red pepper flakes

½ tsp sea salt

½ tsp black pepper

To serve:

2 tbsp fresh parsley, chopped

METHOD

1 Make a few diagonal slashes across the chicken skin, season with the salt and massage it into the chicken, then place the chicken in a large bowl.

2 Place the marinade ingredients in a food processor and blitz.

3 Add marinade to the chicken, and massage thoroughly. Cover and refrigerate for at least 2 hours, or overnight. Remove the chicken from the refrigerator 30 minutes before cooking to allow the meat to come to room temperature. set grill to a medium high heat.

5 Take the chicken out of the marinade, and set the marinade aside for later.

6 Drizzle the chicken with a tablespoon of olive oil, and arrange on a baking sheet in a single layer, skin-side up. Grill the chicken on each side for 10 minutes, until browned, then set aside to rest.

7 Meanwhile, make the sauce. Heat the olive oil in a large pot and add the onions along with the leftover marinade. Cover the pot and cook over a medium heat for 10 minutes, stirring occasionally.

8 After 10 minutes, remove the lid and continue cooking for another 15–20 minutes, until the onions begin to caramelize. Add a splash of water, if needed, to prevent burning.

9 Now add the bell pepper to the onions and cook for 5 minutes, then stir in the garlic cooking for a further 2-3 minutes. Pour in the lemon juice and add the dijon mustard, chicken broth, thyme, bay leaf, red pepper flakes, salt and pepper, and bring to a simmer.

10 Place the chicken, skin-side up, in the sauce. Cover and simmer for 20 minutes, or until the sauce has reduced and the chicken is cooked through.

11 Garnish with freshly chopped parsley and serve.

CALORIES
504

CARBS
7G

PROTEIN
34G

FAT
37G

YOGHURT LEMON CHICKEN

High protein, simple dinner or lunch.

 25 MINS   **SERVES 5**

INGREDIENTS

570g chicken breasts
juice of ½ large lemon
1 tbsp olive oil
140g greek yogurt
1¼ tsp sea salt
black pepper

METHOD

1   In a bowl, combine the lemon juice, olive oil, greek yogurt and sea salt and stir. Add the chicken breasts and stir so that the chicken is covered in the marinade. Cover the bowl and place into the refrigerator for 20 minutes (or up to 1 hour if time allows).

2   When ready to cook the chicken, preheat the oven to 200°C.

3   Remove the chicken from the refrigerator, shake off any excess marinade, and place on a baking dish. Discard any excess marinade.

4   Place the dish into the hot oven for 25 minutes until the chicken is cooked through.

5   When ready to serve, season to taste with black pepper and a little extra salt if required.

CALORIES
183

CARBS
1G

PROTEIN
28G

FAT
6G

GARLIC SRIRACHA PORK STIR FRY

A quick, healthy and filling lunch or dinner.

 10 MINS SERVES 4

INGREDIENTS

450g minced pork

1 tbsp olive oil

2 cloves garlic, crushed

1 onion, sliced

1 aubergine, cut into half moons

1 red pepper, cut into strips

60ml tamari

2 tbsp coconut sugar (or normal sugar)

4 tsp sriracha sauce

200g green beans, cut into 2" (5cm) pieces

20g coriander, chopped (to serve)

METHOD

1   Place the pork into a large pan over a medium-high heat, and brown the pork, breaking it up with a wooden spoon. Transfer to a plate and set aside.

2   Return the pan to a medium heat and warm the olive oil. Add the garlic and onion and sauté for 4 minutes until softened.

3   Increase the heat to medium-high and stir-fry the aubergine and pepper for 2-3 minutes.

4   Meanwhile, in a small bowl combine the tamari, sugar and sriracha and add to the pot, along with the green beans and cooked pork.

5   Sauté until the green beans are bright green and the pork has warmed through.

6   Top with freshly chopped coriander and serve immediately.

CALORIES
382

CARBS
23G

PROTEIN
26G

FAT
23G

SLOW COOKER PULLED CHICKEN

HIGH PROTEIN

A tasty, nutritious dinner for the whole family.

 5 MINS **SERVES 8**

INGREDIENTS

2 tbsp olive oil

10 chicken thighs, boneless & skinless

2 red onions, sliced

2 garlic cloves, minced

2 tsp paprika

120ml water

2 tbsp chipotle paste

240ml tomato sauce (passata)

60ml barbecue sauce

1 tbsp brown sugar

Juice of 1 lime

To serve:

8 tbsp guacamole

8 wholemeal burger buns

METHOD

1   Set the slow cooker to low.

2   Heat 1 tablespoon of the olive oil in a large pan and brown the chicken on both sides before transferring to the slow cooker.

3   Add the remaining oil to the pan and fry the onions for 5 minutes, until softened, then add in the garlic and paprika and cook for a further minute. Transfer the onion mixture into the slow cooker and add the water.

4   Now add the chipotle paste, tomato sauce, barbecue sauce, sugar and lime juice and season with salt and pepper. Stir everything together then cover the slow cooker and cook for 6 hours until the chicken is tender.

5   Using two forks, shred the chicken and mix through the sauce. Serve as a burger with toasted buns and guacamole.

Hob instructions:

Brown then chicken, then remove it from the pan.

Cook the onions and garlic then put the chicken back into the pan, adding the remaining ingredients.

Mix to combine, then cover the pan with a lid and simmer gently for 1-1½ hrs until the chicken is really tender.

CALORIES
485

CARBS
51G

PROTEIN
39G

FAT
15G

Nutritional Advice
Check barbecue sauce for gluten.

HIGH PROTEIN

MARINATED PEANUT SAUCE CHICKEN SKEWERS

An impressive, delicious and healthy dinner.

⏱ **10 MINS**   👤 **SERVES 8**   DF   GF

INGREDIENTS

130g smooth peanut butter

4 garlic cloves, minced

2 tbsp tamari (or soy sauce - contains gluten)

2 tbsp sesame oil

1 tbsp white wine vinegar

2 spring onions, finely chopped

4 tbsp coriander, finely chopped

2 tsp ground ginger

1 tsp salt

1300g boneless skinless chicken thighs, cut into 1 inch pieces (or breast)

12 metal skewers (or bamboo skewers, soaked in water for 30 mins)

METHOD

1   In a bowl, mix together the peanut butter, garlic, tamari, sesame oil, white wine vinegar, onions, coriander, ground ginger and salt.

2   Add the chopped chicken to the peanut sauce, toss until evenly coated. If you have time, allow it to marinate for at least 1 hour or overnight.

3   When ready to cook, heat the oven to 200°C. Place a wire rack on top of a rimmed baking sheet and spray it with a little oil.

4   Thread the marinated chicken onto skewers, lay onto the wire rack and place into the hot oven to bake for 20-25 minutes, until the chicken has cooked through.

5   Serve with sliced cucumber, garnish with chopped peanuts.

To serve and garnish:
75g chopped peanuts, 1 cucumber peeled & sliced

CALORIES
391

CARBS
24G

PROTEIN
39G

FAT
7G

HIGH PROTEIN

TIKKA MASALA SKEWERS

The perfect fakeaway! High in protein, this dinner is filling and nutritious.

⏱ **20 MINS**   👤 **SERVES 6**

INGREDIENTS

2 tbsp tikka masala curry paste

430g Greek yogurt

salt & pepper

900g skinless/boneless chicken thighs, cut into pieces (or breast if preferred)

15g coriander

2 tsp coconut sugar (or sugar of choice)

1½ inch (4cm) ginger, finely chopped

2 garlic cloves, chopped

60ml + 2 tbsp. olive oil

1 lime

1 cucumber, sliced

2 tbsp coriander, chopped

METHOD

1   If using wooden skewers, soak in water for 30 mins.

2   Combine the tikka masala paste with 285g of yogurt and season with salt and pepper. Coat the chicken in the marinade, then cover and refrigerate for 15 minutes.

3   Coriander sauce - Place the coriander, sugar, ginger, garlic, 60ml of olive oil and ½ the lime juice in a food processor and blitz until smooth. Stir in remaining 145g of yogurt, season with salt and pepper and set aside.

4   In the meanwhile, toss the cucumber with the remaining lime juice, season with salt and pepper and set aside.

5   Heat the 2 tablespoons of olive oil in a non-stick pan over a medium/high heat. Thread the chicken onto the skewers, place into the hot pan and cook for 8-10 minutes, turning every few minutes until cooked through on both sides.

6   Serve the skewers with coriander yogurt sauce and cucumber salad, and garnish with freshly chopped coriander.

CALORIES
390

CARBS
13G

PROTEIN
39G

FAT
21G

BEEF KEBABS WITH SMOKY CHIMICHURRI

Restaurant quality! A high protein, low calorie dinner.

 30 MINS SERVES 8

INGREDIENTS

Bamboo or metal skewers
Skewers:
900g beef sirloin (or cut of choice) cut into 1½ inch (4cm) cubes
300g cherry tomatoes
2 red onions, cut into wedges

Marinade:
2 tbsp olive oil
2 tbsp lime juice, plus zest of one lime
2 cloves garlic, minced
1 tsp onion powder
1 tsp dried oregano
1 tsp ground cumin
1 tsp salt
½ tsp black pepper

Smoky chimichurri sauce:
20g coriander
120ml olive oil
2 tbsp lime juice
1 small onion, chopped
1 garlic clove
1 tsp ground coriander
½ tsp smoked paprika
½ tsp salt
1 jalapeño - skip this ingredient for a mild sauce

METHOD

1 Soak 8 bamboo skewers in warm water for 30 minutes, or use metal skewers.

2 Place the diced beef into a zip lock bag and add in the marinade ingredients. Mix well until coated evenly and set aside to marinate.

3 Preheat the grill.

4 In the meantime, make the chimichurri sauce by placing all the ingredients in a food processor. Blitz repeatedly until the onion is minced well. Place in a small bowl and set aside.

5 Assemble the skewers alternating the cubes of beef, cherry tomato and onion slices. Place about 3-4 pieces of beef on each skewer.

6 Grill the skewers over medium high heat, rotating until the steak is nicely charred and cooked to your preference.

7 Serve the beef skewers with the smoky chimichurri sauce.

CALORIES
233

CARBS
4G

PROTEIN
34G

FAT
9G

TUNA PASTA BAKE

A very tasty, nutritious family dinner.

 10 MINS  **SERVES 6**

INGREDIENTS

300g dried pasta

1 tsp olive oil

2 courgettes, diced

5 spring onions, sliced

½ tsp smoked paprika

½ tsp garlic powder

400ml vegetable broth

100g frozen peas

100g spinach

juice of ½ lemon

150g low-fat cream cheese

2× 160g tins tuna, drained

40g grated cheddar cheese

METHOD

1   Preheat the oven to 190°C.

2   Cook the pasta according to instructions on the packaging.

3   While the pasta is cooking, grease a large frying pan with the olive oil and place over a medium heat. Add the courgettes and spring onions and sauté for 5 minutes.

4   Next stir in the paprika and garlic powder, mix to combine then add the broth, peas, spinach and lemon juice.

5   Cook for 2-3 minutes until the spinach has wilted, then stir in the cream cheese.

6   Break up the tuna into flakes in a bowl. Drain the pasta and add it to the pan of vegetables along with the tuna flakes.

7   Stir together so that everything is well coated. Place the pasta mixture into a large oven-proof dish, sprinkle over the grated cheese and place the dish into the hot oven for 15 minutes.

8   Remove the pasta bake from the oven and serve immediately.

CALORIES
416

CARBS
44G

PROTEIN
23G

FAT
16G

CREAMY SPICY SPAGHETTI

A filling dinner for the family and quick to make.

 5 MINS SERVES 4

INGREDIENTS

300g spaghetti

1 tbsp olive oil

2 tbsp chilli paste

1 tbsp tomato paste

300g canned diced tomatoes

240ml water

½ tsp salt

3 egg yolks

45g parmesan cheese, grated

Optional:

½ tsp ground black pepper

3 garlic cloves, chopped

METHOD

1   Cook the spaghetti according to the instructions on packaging.

2   Meanwhile, heat the olive oil in a pot over a medium/high heat and cook the garlic for 1-2 minutes, until fragrant.

3   Now add chilli paste and tomato paste and cook for a further 30 seconds.

4   Add the diced tomatoes, water, and season with salt. Mix together to combine, bring to a gentle simmer and allow to cook for 3 minutes.

5   In a separate bowl, whisk together the egg yolks, parmesan cheese and optional black pepper.

6   Add the pasta to the sauce together with the egg & parmesan cheese mixture and cook for a further 2-3 minutes, until the sauce becomes smooth and creamy.

7   Finally add the cooked spaghetti to the pot and stir until the pasta is completely covered in the creamy sauce. Serve immediately.

CALORIES
414

CARBS
59G

PROTEIN
17G

FAT
12G

CHICKEN TIKKA ALFREDO

A full of flavour dinner the family will love.

 20 MINS SERVES 6

INGREDIENTS

For the chicken:

680g boneless skinless chicken thighs

140g Greek yogurt

3 cloves garlic, minced

1 tbsp ginger, minced

1½ tsp garam masala

½ tsp ground cumin

½ tsp ground coriander

½ tsp salt

¼ tsp cayenne pepper

cooking spray

For the sauce & pasta:

3 tbsp ghee or unsalted butter

1 large onion, finely chopped

5 cloves garlic, minced

2 tbsp fresh ginger, minced

2 tbsp garam masala

1½ tsp ground cumin

1½ tsp ground coriander

1 tsp ground cardamom

170g tomato paste

Optional:

1-2 jalapeño or chilli peppers, seeded, & minced

420ml water

2 tsp honey

240g oat cream (or double cream if preferred)

salt

450g spaghetti

fresh coriander, for garnish

METHOD

1 Place the chicken thighs into a large bowl. Add the Greek yogurt, garlic, ginger, and spices, and stir until the chicken is completely coated. Cover the bowl with a lid and transfer to the refrigerator to marinate for at least 30 minutes, or up to 2 hours.

2 In a large, heavy-bottomed pot, melt the ghee / butter over a medium-high heat. Add the onions, garlic, ginger, and peppers and cook for 8-10 minutes, stirring occasionally, until the vegetables are soft and beginning to brown on the edges.

3 Reduce the heat to medium and stir in spices, cooking for 2-3 minutes until very fragrant. Stir in tomato paste and cook until dark red, a further 2-3 minutes.

4 Whisk in the water, ensuring there are no clumps, then add honey. Take the pot off heat and stir in cream. Use an immersion blender, or carefully pour the sauce into a traditional blender, and blend the sauce until smooth. Return the sauce to the pot.

5 Position an oven rack 5-6" from the grill and heat the grill. Line a baking sheet with foil and grease with cooking spray.

6 Transfer the pieces of marinated chicken to the baking sheet, ensuring some yogurt remains on the chicken. Grill the chicken, flipping once halfway through, until cooked through and charred, 18-20 minutes.

7 Transfer the chicken to a cutting board and let it cool a little, before roughly chopping and adding to the sauce.

8 Meanwhile, cook the spaghetti to al dente according to package directions. Drain and set aside.

9 Bring the sauce to a gentle simmer, add the cooked chicken and pasta. Toss everything together and continue cooking for 2-3 minutes until everything is warmed through.

10 Garnish the pasta with coriander before serving.

CALORIES
571

CARBS
67G

PROTEIN
32G

FAT
17G

HIGH
PROTEIN

TURKEY MEATLOAF

A tasty, high protein dinner or make for lunch the next day.

 15 MINS   **SERVES 6**

INGREDIENTS

olive oil cooking spray

1 tbsp olive oil

1 large yellow onion, chopped

salt & pepper

3 cloves garlic, minced

1 tbsp rosemary, finely chopped

1 tsp thyme leaves, chopped

900g turkey mince

80g breadcrumbs

120ml milk

2 tbsp worcestershire sauce

1 egg

80g tomato ketchup

2 tbsp coconut sugar (or regular sugar)

METHOD

1   Preheat the oven to 160°C. Lightly grease a large deep baking dish with cooking spray.

2   Heat the olive oil in a large frying pan over a medium heat, add the onion and cook for 5 minutes until soft. Season with salt and pepper, then stir in the garlic and herbs. Cook for 1 minute until fragrant, then remove from heat and set aside to cool slightly.

3   Mix the turkey, breadcrumbs, milk, worcestershire sauce, egg, and cooked vegetables together in a large bowl until well combined. Season with salt and pepper.

4   Add the turkey mixture to the prepared baking dish, and form the meat mixture into a loaf shape.

5   Add the tomato ketchup and sugar to a small bowl, mix to combine and brush over the loaf.

6   Place the dish into the hot oven and bake for around 1 hour 20 minutes, until the meatloaf reaches an internal temperature of 71°C.

7   Serve with your choice of sides.

CALORIES
354

CARBS
20G

PROTEIN
32G

FAT
17G

LOW CALORIE

ONE POT SPANISH CHICKEN & RICE

An easy, delicious and filling dinner for the family.

🕐 **15 MINS** 👤 **SERVES 4**

INGREDIENTS

1 tbsp olive oil

450g skinless boneless chicken thighs cut into pieces

½ tsp salt

½ tsp black pepper

½ medium onion, diced

1 red bell pepper

diced 2 cloves garlic, minced

160g long grain white rice, rinsed

½ tbsp smoked paprika

360ml chicken broth

240ml tomato sauce (passata)

pinch of saffron

70g green olives

8g coriander, chopped

1 lemon, cut into wedges

METHOD

1   Heat the olive oil in a large pan over a medium heat. Add the chicken and season with salt and pepper. Cook for 5-6 minutes until slightly brown.

2   Add in the onion, red bell pepper and garlic and cook for a few minutes until they slightly soften.

3   Now add the rice, stir to combine and cook for a further 1-2 minutes.

4   Next add in the paprika, chicken broth and tomato sauce. Bring to a boil, then turn down the heat to low.

5   Add the saffron, cover the pan with a lid and cook gently for 25 minutes until the rice is ready.

6   Season with a little more salt and pepper to taste, and stir through the olives and coriander. Serve with lemon wedges!

CALORIES
370

CARBS
43G

PROTEIN
27G

FAT
11G

GREEK MEATBALLS WITH TOMATO SALAD & TZATZIKI

HIGH PROTEIN

Simple to make! A delicious, healthy meal for the family.

🕙 **10 MINS**   👤 **SERVES 6**

INGREDIENTS

For the meatballs:
900g 5% fat beef mince
1 onion, grated
3 cloves garlic, minced
2 tsp salt
1 tsp ground pepper
2 tsp ground cumin
1 tsp ground cinnamon
2 tsp dried oregano
8g parsley, minced
2 eggs
60g panko breadcrumbs

Tomato salad:
4 tomatoes, chopped
1 tsp salt
½ red onion, thinly sliced
4 tbsp white wine vinegar
2 tsp coconut sugar
2 tbsp. fresh dill, chopped

Tzatziki sauce:
1 cucumber, grated
1 tsp salt
285g Greek yogurt
2 tbsp lemon juice
3 tbsp fresh dill, chopped

To serve:
4 pittas, toasted

METHOD

1   Preheat the air fryer or the oven to 190°C.

2   In a large bowl, combine all the ingredients for the meatballs, mix together using your hands. Roll the beef mixture into even-sized balls the size of a walnut.

   Air fryer - Working in batches, cook the meatballs in the air fryer basket in a single layer for 8-10 minutes, or until cooked through.

   Oven - Place meatballs on a parchment lined tray and cook for up to 15 mins.

3   In the meantime, add the tomatoes to a large bowl with the salt and stir through the remaining ingredients. Refrigerate until ready to serve.

4   For the tzatziki sauce, place the grated cucumber into a medium bowl with the salt. Set aside for 2 minutes, then drain off any excess water. Mix in the remaining ingredients, then cover and refrigerate until ready to serve.

5   When the meatballs have finished cooking, divide equally onto plates and serve with a portion of the tomato salad, tzatziki and toasted pitta bread.

CALORIES
562

CARBS
53G

PROTEIN
45G

FAT
19G

FAMILY CHICKEN RATATOUILLE RICE

A super healthy, filling family meal.

 15 MINS SERVES 4

INGREDIENTS

3 tbsp olive oil, divided

450g boneless, skinless chicken thighs, cut into 1-inch pieces

½ tsp salt, divided

ground black pepper

1 onion, chopped

4 cloves garlic, chopped

1 aubergine, chopped

2 courgettes, chopped

1 red bell pepper, chopped

140g long-grain white rice

400g can diced tomatoes

240ml chicken broth

1 tsp dried thyme

1 tsp dried parsley

METHOD

1   Place a large pot over medium-high heat and add 1 tablespoon of olive oil. Toss the chicken with ¼ teaspoon of salt and black pepper, then add to the pot in an even layer.

2   Cook the chicken for 3-4 minutes, stirring occasionally, or until the chicken has lightly browned on all sides. Once cooked, transfer the chicken to a plate and set aside.

3   In the same pot, reduce the heat to medium and add the remaining 2 tablespoons of olive oil. Add the onion, garlic, thyme, parsley, remaining ¼ teaspoon salt and black pepper. Cook, stirring often, for 3-5 minutes, or until the onions are translucent.

4   Add the aubergine, courgette and bell pepper. Cook for 5-7 minutes, stirring often, until the courgette and aubergine have started to soften.

5   Now add the rice, diced tomatoes with their juices and broth, and stir to combine. Return the chicken to the pot and stir to combine.

6   Then reduce the heat to low, cover the pot with a lid and cook for about 30 minutes, stirring occasionally, until all of the liquid has been absorbed. Serve immediately.

CALORIES
445

CARBS
48G

PROTEIN
29G

FAT
16G

Nutritional Advice
Check broth for gluten..

LOW CALORIE

ONE POT BEEF & VEGETABLE PASTA

A quick, wholesome lunch or dinner.

 10 MINS   **SERVES 5**   (DF)

INGREDIENTS

450g 95% lean beef mince

1 onion, chopped

2 celery, chopped

1 green bell pepper, chopped

2 tsp worcestershire sauce

1 tsp salt, optional

¼ tsp black pepper

½ tsp dried basil

225g dry pasta of choice

400g can kidney beans, drained & rinsed

400g can chopped tomatoes

180ml cup water

1 beef bouillon / stock cube

4 tbsp chopped basil, to serve (optional)

METHOD

1 Place a large pot over medium heat, add the beef mince, onion, celery and green bell pepper and sauté until the vegetables are tender and the meat is no longer pink. Drain off any excess liquid.

2 Add the worcestershire sauce, salt, pepper, basil, pasta, beans, tomatoes, water and bouillon cube and stir to combine.

3 Bring to a boil, then reduce the heat; cover the pot with a lid, and simmer for 20-25 minutes or until pasta is tender, stirring occasionally.

4 Serve the pasta topped with a garnish of fresh basil.

CALORIES
493

CARBS
53G

PROTEIN
24G

FAT
19G

CRISPY BAKED
CHICKEN NUGGETS

A tasty and healthy recipe the whole family will love!

 20 MINS   SERVES 4

INGREDIENTS

90g panko breadcrumbs

2 tbsp olive oil

1 tsp salt

1 tsp black pepper

1 tsp onion powder

1 tsp paprika

½ tsp garlic powder

¼ tsp cayenne pepper

2 eggs

2 tbsp unsweetened almond milk

450g boneless skinless chicken breast, cut into cubes

METHOD

1   Preheat the oven to 200°C.

2   Place the breadcrumbs on a large baking sheet and spray with a little olive oil. Place in the oven and bake for 2 minutes, stir the breadcrumbs and return to the oven to bake for a further 2-3 minutes, until the breadcrumbs are golden brown.

3   Transfer the breadcrumbs to a bowl and add the salt, black pepper, onion powder, paprika, garlic powder and cayenne pepper. Set aside.

4   In a separate shallow bowl, whisk together the eggs and almond milk. Set aside.

5   Line the large baking sheet with baking paper and place a wire rack over it. Grease the rack with olive oil.

6   Dip each piece of chicken into the egg/milk mixture, then into the breadcrumb mixture, until evenly coated. Place the chicken directly onto the wire rack.

7   Generously spray the tops of the chicken nuggets with olive oil spray. Place the chicken into the hot oven to bake in the oven for 15-20 minutes until cooked through and golden.

CALORIES
325

CARBS
17G

PROTEIN
32G

FAT
13G

LOW
CALORIE

SLOW COOKED FAJITA CHICKEN

Tasty, low calorie simple recipe with just 4 main ingredients.

 5 MINS  SERVES 6

INGREDIENTS

680g chicken breast
1 large onion, sliced
2 bell peppers, sliced
450g jar salsa
Juice of 1 lime
salt & pepper

METHOD

1   Add the chicken, onions, peppers, salsa, and salt to a slow cooker. Stir well to combine.

2   Cook on a high heat setting for 4 hours or low heat setting for 6 hours, until the chicken and vegetables are tender.

3   Once cooked, remove the chicken and place on a cutting board. Shred the chicken, with two forks and place back into the slow cooker. Add in the lime juice and mix everything well to combine.

4   Season to taste, with salt and pepper.

CALORIES
177

CARBS
10G

PROTEIN
27G

FAT
3G

HARISSA CHICKEN
WITH CHICKPEAS & SWEET POTATOES

Delicious, healthy tray bake meal for the family.

 15 MINS   **SERVES 6**

INGREDIENTS

680g chicken breasts

4 tbsp olive oil

1 lemon, juice & zest + 1 lemon, sliced

2 tbsp harissa paste

1 tbsp honey

salt & pepper

2 sweet potatoes, cut into chunks

1 red onion, sliced

1x 400g can chickpeas, drained

80g crumbled feta

60g green olives

METHOD

1   Preheat the oven to 220C.

2   Place the chicken breasts onto a baking tray and add 2 tablespoons of the olive oil, along with the lemon juice, lemon zest, harissa paste, and honey.

3   Season with salt and pepper and toss together until the chicken is well coated.

4   Add the sweet potatoes, onion and chickpeas to the tray, and toss with the remaining 2 tablespoons of olive oil.

5   Arrange everything in an even layer, lay the lemon slices over the chicken and place the tray into the hot oven.

6   Roast for 40-45 minutes, tossing halfway through, until the chicken is cooked through and the potatoes are golden.

7   Serve warm, topped with the feta cheese and olives.

CALORIES
378

CARBS
25G

PROTEIN
32G

FAT
17G

SLOW COOKER LAMB ROGAN JOSH

Tasty, nutritious dinner for the family.

 20 MINS SERVES 4

INGREDIENTS

680g lamb neck fillet
1 white onion, sliced
2 tbsp olive oil

Paste:

3 tbsp tomato paste
3 garlic cloves, minced
2 tsp paprika
1 tsp smoked paprika
1½ tsp cumin
1½ tsp garam masala
1 tsp ground ginger
½ tsp ground black pepper
1 tsp salt
1 tsp chilli powder
1 tbsp olive oil
1 beef stock cube, crumbled

Sauce:

250g natural yogurt
1 tbsp coriander, chopped
½ tsp sugar
1 red chilli, seeds removed, finely chopped
400g tomato sauce
60ml water
2 bay leaves
1 tbsp cardamom pods
1 cinnamon stick

METHOD

1 In a large bowl, mix together the ingredients to form a paste.

2 Prepare the lamb fillet by removing any sinew and cutting into 1 - 1.5 inch chunks. Add the lamb to the paste and stir to coat. Cover the bowl and set aside in the refrigerator and marinate for at least 30 mins, or ideally overnight.

3 Heat a large frying pan over a medium/high heat and sear the marinated lamb, along with the onions until brown. Transfer to the slow cooker.

4 In another bowl mix together the coriander, yoghurt, sugar and chopped chilli and gradually stir in the tomato sauce and water.

5 Pour the sauce over the lamb and onions, then add the bay leaves, cardamom pods and cinnamon stick and ensure they are submerged in the sauce.

6 Cover with a lid and cook on low for 6 hours or high for 3.5 hours.

7 When ready to serve remove the bay leaves, cinnamon stick and pods.

CALORIES
342

CARBS
10G

PROTEIN
27G

FAT
22G

SLOW COOKER BEEF ROAST

Delicious melt in your mouth beef.

 10 MINS   SERVES 8

INGREDIENTS

2 tbsp olive oil
1.6kg braising beef steak
2 tsp salt
1 tsp black pepper
4 cloves garlic, thinly sliced
1 onion, cut into large chunks
4 carrots, peeled and cut into 1-inch pieces
3 stalks celery, cut into 1-inch pieces
680g baby potatoes, quartered
2 sprigs fresh rosemary
2 sprigs fresh thyme
2 bay leaves
720ml beef broth
240ml red wine

For gravy:
2 tbsp cornstarch
3 tbsp water

METHOD

1   Heat the olive oil in a large frying pan over a medium-high heat. Season both sides of the beef steak with salt and pepper, place into the hot pan and sear for 4-5 minutes, browning each side of the roasting joint. Transfer the roast to the bowl of the slow cooker.

2   Add the garlic, onion, carrots, celery, potatoes, rosemary, thyme, and bay leaves to the slow cooker. Pour over the beef broth and red wine, cover with a lid and cook on LOW for 8 hours or on HIGH for 6 hours.

3   Once cooked, remove the sprigs of rosemary, thyme, and the bay leaves. Then remove the roast and shred the meat using 2 forks.

4   Mix the cornstarch and water together in a small bowl and stir to combine. Add the mixture to the slow cooker and stir everything together until the gravy starts to thicken.

5   Serve the meat and vegetables on a platter pouring over some of the gravy.

CALORIES
410

CARBS
22G

PROTEIN
23G

FAT
26G

HIGH PROTEIN

PORK MEATBALLS IN TOMATO SAUCE

Healthy, nutritious, low calorie snack.

 10 MINS **SERVES 4**

INGREDIENTS

400g lean pork mince
1 clove garlic, minced
1 yellow onion, chopped
480ml passata
2 tbsp olive oil
Salt & pepper

Optional:
15g parsley leaf

METHOD

1   Place the pork in a medium bowl, season with salt and pepper. Add in the garlic and use your hands to mix thoroughly. Using 1 tablespoon of mince, form meatballs, roughly the size of a walnut.

2   Heat 1 tablespoon of olive oil in a large pan and cook the meatballs, turning occasionally, for 10 minutes or until browned and cooked through. Then take off the heat and set aside.

3   In the same pan, heat the remaining oil and cook the onion for 3-4 minutes until soft.

4   Place the meatballs back into the pan and add the passata. Season with salt and pepper, bring to a boil and then reduce the heat.

5   Simmer for 10 minutes, garnish with parsley (optional) and serve.

CALORIES
320

CARBS
10G

PROTEIN
20G

FAT
23TG

SLOW COOKER CHICKEN TINGA

Delicious, filling dinner which plenty leftover for lunch.

 5 MINS   SERVES 6

INGREDIENTS

400g can chopped tomatoes

4 chipotle peppers in adobo sauce

1 diced yellow onion

1½ tbsp coconut sugar (or white sugar if preferred)

1 tbsp garlic, fresh

2 tsp smoked paprika

2 tsp ground cumin

1 tsp dried oregano

juice of 1 lime

900g chicken breast

*1-2 tsp Chipotle paste can be used as an alternative to peppers

METHOD

1   Add all the ingredients to the slow cooker bowl and mix together. Nestle the chicken breasts into the sauce.

2   Cover with the lid and cook on HIGH for 4 hours, or on LOW for 6 hours.

3   Remove the chicken breasts into a bowl, and using forks, gently pull the chicken apart to shred the chicken.

4   Using an immersion blender, blend the tinga sauce until smooth.

5   Now add the shredded chicken back into the sauce and thoroughly mix together. Cook on low for an additional 6-10 minutes to warm through.

6   Enjoy with any sides or create in the Chicken Tinga Bowl, and Cheesy Chicken Tinga Quesadillas recipes (see lunch recipes).

CALORIES
474

CARBS
10G

PROTEIN
22G

FAT
40G

FISH CURRY

Simple, easy, high protein dinner.

⏱ **5 MINS**   👤 **SERVES 4**   DF   GF

INGREDIENTS

1 medium yellow onion, chopped

3 tbsp green curry paste

400ml can coconut milk

600g white fish fillets (such as cod)

1 tbsp olive oil

360g frozen vegetable mix

METHOD

1   Heat the oil in a wok or high sided frying pan over high heat. Add the chopped onion and cook for 3-4 minutes, then add the curry paste and cook, stirring, for 1 more minute.

2   Add the coconut milk and bring to a boil.

3   Reduce the heat to medium-low and add the fish and frozen vegetables.

4   Simmer for 15 minutes, until fish is cooked and the vegetables have warmed through. Serve immediately.

 CALORIES 351

 CARBS 14G

 PROTEIN 29G

 FAT 20G

Nutritional Advice
Please check curry paste for gluten. Dairy free, freezer friendly, high protein.

Dinner
96

HIGH PROTEIN

COD FISH CAKES WITH MINT PEAS

Tasty fish cakes you'll never buy shop made again!

 20 MINS **SERVES 4** *DF*

INGREDIENTS

900g potatoes, peeled & cut into medium chunks
2 tsp mustard powder
4 anchovies, finely chopped
5 spring onions, finely sliced
2 tsp capers
1½ tbsp tarragon, chopped
560g skinless cod, cut into cubes
8 tsp wholemeal flour (or all purpose if preferred)
2 eggs
90g ground almonds

For the vegetables:
320g frozen peas
320g leeks, halved & finely sliced
2 tbsp finely chopped mint

METHOD

1 Heat the oven to 180°C. Prepare a baking sheet lined with baking paper.

2 Bring a pan of water to the boil and cook the potatoes for 15-20 minutes until tender. Drain well, then return to the pan and mash with the mustard, anchovies, green onions, capers and tarragon until well combined. Now stir through the raw cod.

3 Shape the mixture into 8 even-sized fish cakes, then coat lightly in the flour.

4 Beat the eggs in a shallow bowl and coat the fish cakes in the egg mixture. Now coat each of the fish cakes with ½ tablespoon of the ground almonds, and place on the baking sheet.

5 Place the fish cakes into the hot oven to bake for 20 minutes until golden brown, turning each fish cake over halfway through.

6 Meanwhile, place the peas and leeks in a pot and cover with boiling water. Cook on medium-high for 10 minutes, then drain and stir through the mint.

CALORIES
519

CARBS
65G

PROTEIN
30G

FAT
11G

STEAMED COCONUT FISH & JASMINE RICE

A fresh, high protein healthy dinner.

 15 MINS **SERVES 4**

INGREDIENTS

4x 170g white fish fillets
(e.g. cod or halibut)

320g cooked Jasmine rice

1 lemon, slices

basil, thinly sliced

red chilli, sliced

2 carrots, cut into
matchsticks

1 red bell pepper, sliced

For the marinade:

200g can light coconut
milk

1 shallot, chopped

4 tbsp ginger, chopped

1 lemongrass stalk, peeled
& chopped into pieces

1 turmeric root, chopped

1 tsp coriander

zest from 1 lime

juice from ½ lime

4 tbsp basil

salt & pepper

METHOD

1 Set the oven to 200°C.

2 Place all marinade ingredients in a food processor and blitz until smooth, season to taste with sea salt & pepper.

3 Place the fish in a bowl, pour half of the marinade over the fish, and set aside in the refrigerator to marinate for 15-20 minutes.

4 Meanwhile, prepare 4 large sheets of parchment paper, about 16.5"x22" (40x55cm), and fold each sheet in half.

5 Open up the parchment and in the centre along the crease, add 80g of cooked rice. Top the rice with 2 lemon slices, basil and red chilli, and then place the fish on top.

6 Spread the remaining marinade over the fish. Place the carrots and bell pepper alongside the fish.

7 Fold the parchment parcel up, and roll the edges until sealed.

8 Place the parchment parcels on a baking sheet and bake in the hot oven for 15-20 minutes.

9 Serve immediately, taking care when opening the parcels to allow the steam to escape.

CALORIES
337

CARBS
33G

PROTEIN
37G

FAT
6G

Savoury Snacks

SWEET POTATO PANCAKES

High fibre, filling snack or light lunch.

⏱ **10 MINS**   👤 **SERVES 4**   Ⓥ   ⒹⒻ

INGREDIENTS

300g sweet potato, grated
½ small onion, grated
2 eggs
3 heaped tbsp. all purpose flour
2 tbsp olive oil
½ tsp sweet paprika

Optional:
1 clove garlic, crushed

METHOD

1   Place the grated sweet potato and onion in a large bowl. Add in the eggs, flour, season with salt and pepper, optional crushed garlic, as well as the paprika. Mix thoroughly.

2   Heat the oil in a pan, and add a heaped tablespoon of the batter per 1 pancake (makes around 16).

3   Fry for around 3 minutes on medium heat, then flip and fry for another 1-2 minutes.

4   Serve with your favourite toppings (see ideas below).

tomato / cream / lamb's lettuce or parsley / onion
sliced cherry tomatoes / feta cheese / rocket / onion
hummus / avocado / tomato / onion

 CALORIES 199

 CARBS 25G

 PROTEIN 5G

 FAT 9G

LOW CALORIE

HEALTHY PINWHEEL SANDWICHES

A quick, filling lunch. Perfect to take on the go!

 10 MINS **SERVES 1**

INGREDIENTS

2 multigrain flour tortillas

4 tbsp hummus

30g sliced turkey ham

1 handful baby spinach

4 tbsp red bell pepper, thinly sliced

2 tbsp grated carrots

4 tbsp salad leaves

4 tbsp dressing of choice

METHOD

1   Spread the tortilla with hummus and top with sliced turkey ham, spinach, bell pepper, carrots, and salad leaves.

2   Roll up each wrap and slice into 1" (2.5cm) rounds.

3   Serve with dressing of choice.

CALORIES
52

CARBS
66G

PROTEIN
19G

FAT
23G

GOATS CHEESE STUFFED DATES WITH HONEY & NUTS

Impress your guests!
A delightfully elegant snack where sweet meets savoury.

 15 MINS **SERVES 15**

INGREDIENTS

15 medjool dates, pitted halved

100g goat cheese, soft

4 tbsp walnuts

2 tbsp pistachios

1 tsp honey, to serve

METHOD

1 Smear a small amount of goat cheese into each date half.

2 Place the walnuts and pistachios into the goat cheese, allowing 1-2 nuts per date, depending on the size.

3 Serve the dates with a drizzle of honey

CALORIES
103

CARBS
19G

PROTEIN
2G

FAT
3G

LOW CALORIE

EGG BROCCOLI & HAM MUFFINS

A filling tasty snack at around 100 calories and 10g of protein.
Also great for kids!

⏱ **5 MINS**   👤 **SERVES 6**   🅳🅵   🅶🅵

INGREDIENTS

½ broccoli

1 clove garlic, minced

5 eggs

pinch of chilli flakes, optional

4 slices ham, chopped

30g grated cheese

METHOD

1   Preheat the oven to 180°C.

2   Place the broccoli in a pot of boiling water and cook for approximately 3 minutes. Strain and cut into small pieces.

3   Beat the eggs in a medium size bowl, add the minced garlic and season with salt and pepper, and chilli flakes if using.

4   Grease a 6-mould muffin tray with oil or butter, and fill the moulds with evenly divided broccoli, ham, and grated cheese.

5   Pour the beaten eggs into the moulds and bake in the oven for 10-15 minutes, or until eggs have set.

6   Vegetarian option: Replace the ham with feta cheese, Goats cheese or your favourite vegetables.

CALORIES
102

CARBS
4G

PROTEIN
10G

FAT
6G

BACON, SPINACH & EGG CUPS

Simple, high protein breakfast.

 5 MINS SERVES 5

INGREDIENTS

6 slices smoked bacon
6 eggs
30g baby spinach
salt & pepper

METHOD

1   Preheat the oven to 190°C. Prepare a silicone muffin cup tray.

2   Line the bottom and sides of each cup with a slice of bacon, cutting the bacon into strips if required to ensure coverage

3   Now press 4-5 spinach leaves into the bottom of each cup. Then crack one egg into each cup and season with a little salt and pepper.

4   Place the muffin tray into the hot oven, on the middle rack and cook for about 15 minutes, or longer depending on how set you like the eggs cooked.

5   Remove the muffin tin from the oven and allow it to cool slightly before serving.

6   Leftovers can be stored in an airtight container in the refrigerator for 3-4 days.

CALORIES
183

CARBS
1G

PROTEIN
10G

FAT
15G

LOW
CALORIE

TAHINI BREAD

A simple, low calorie nutritious snack, full of good fats.

 5 MINS SERVES 13

INGREDIENTS

4 eggs
1 tsp baking soda
240g tahini
1 tsp sesame seeds

METHOD

1 Preheat the oven to 180°C. Line a bread tin with baking paper.

2 Place the eggs, baking soda and tahini in a bowl and mix with a hand mixer until well combined.

3 Pour the batter into the bread tin and sprinkle over the sesame seeds. Place the tin into the hot oven to bake for 30 minutes.

4 Once baked, remove the tin from the oven and place on a wire rack to cool completely before slicing and serving.

CALORIES
133

CARBS
4G

PROTEIN
5G

FAT
12G

CHEESY BROCCOLI MUFFINS

The perfect go-to snack or lunch option.

 10 MINS SERVES 12

INGREDIENTS

180g wholewheat flour (or all purpose flour)

1 tsp baking powder

1 tsp baking soda

1 tsp garlic powder

1 tsp onion powder

200g finely chopped broccoli florets

115g grated cheddar cheese, divided

180ml milk

125g ricotta cheese

2 eggs

6 tbsp. olive oil

METHOD

1 Preheat the oven to 220°C. Line a 12 hole muffin pan with liners, or prepare a silicone muffin pan.

2 In a medium bowl, combine the whole wheat flour, baking powder, baking soda, garlic powder, and onion powder. Add the broccoli, and 90g of cheddar cheese and toss to coat.

3 In a separate bowl, combine the milk, ricotta cheese, eggs and olive oil. Pour into the flour mixture and stir until just combined.

4 Fill each muffin cup about ⅔ full with batter. Sprinkle the remaining cheddar cheese on top of each muffin.

5 Place the muffin pan into the hot oven and bake for about 15 minutes, until a toothpick inserted into the centre of the muffin comes out clean.

6 Remove the muffins from the oven and place on a wire rack to cool.

7 Store the muffins in an airtight container on the counter top for 3-4 days.

CALORIES
194

CARBS
14G

PROTEIN
7G

FAT
13G

CHICKEN & SUNDRIED TOMATO MUFFINS

 15 MINS  SERVES 9

INGREDIENTS

180g all purpose flour

1 tsp baking powder

pinch of salt

pinch of black pepper

50ml olive oil

100ml milk

3 eggs

150g cooked chicken, chopped

100g sun-dried tomatoes, chopped

60g ricotta cheese

6 leaves of basil, sliced

METHOD

1 Preheat your oven to 180°C. Prepare a muffin tin with paper liners or use the silicone muffin tray.

2 Mix the flour, baking powder, salt & pepper in a bowl. Add the olive oil, milk and eggs and whisk to combine.

3 Fold in the cooked chicken, sun-dried tomatoes, ricotta and basil. Mix well and divide the batter equally between 10 muffin cases.

4 Bake the muffins in the preheated oven for 15 minutes. Once baked, place the muffins onto a wire rack and serve warm or cool for later.

5 Store leftover muffins in an airtight container at room temperature for 2-3 days.

CALORIES
210

CARBS
24G

PROTEIN
11G

FAT
9G

CHICKEN & EGG SALAD

High protein, light lunch or use as breakfast or snack.

 5 MINS SERVES 4

INGREDIENTS

300g chicken breasts
3 eggs, hard boiled
2 tbsp low fat mayonnaise
1 tsp curry powder

Optional:
salad leaves
1 tbsp chives, chopped

Ideally served with
wholegrain bread.

METHOD

1   Preheat the oven to 180°C. Line a baking sheet
with baking paper.

2   Place the chicken onto the baking sheet and bake
for about 20 minutes, or until the chicken has
cooked through.

3   Meanwhile, place the eggs into a pan and cover
with cold water. Bring the water to the boil and boil
the eggs for 8 minutes. Run under cold running
water then when cool enough to handle, peel the
eggs and set aside.

4   Once the chicken and eggs have cooked and
cooled, cut both into bite-sized pieces and place
in a bowl.

5   Add the mayonnaise, curry powder and optional
chives, and mix until well combined.

CALORIES
192

CARBS
1G

PROTEIN
22G

FAT
11G

PUMPKIN SPICE BREAD

Utterly delicious and quick to prepare!

 15 MINS **SERVES 12**

INGREDIENTS

210g all-purpose flour

100g coconut sugar (or alternative sugar)

1 tsp baking soda

¾ tsp salt

2 large eggs

340g pumpkin puree

60ml melted coconut oil

60ml maple syrup

1 tsp vanilla extract

1 tbsp ground cinnamon

2 tsp ground ginger

1 tsp ground nutmeg

¾ tsp ground cardamom

¾ tsp ground cloves

Topping:

4 tbsp chopped pecans

METHOD

1   Preheat the oven to 160°C. Grease a 9x5-inch (23x13cm) loaf pan.

2   In a large bowl, whisk dry ingredients together, the flour, sugar, baking soda, salt, and spices.

3   In a medium bowl, whisk wet ingredients together, the eggs, pumpkin puree, coconut oil, maple syrup and vanilla extract.

4   Pour the wet ingredients into dry ingredients and whisk until combined. Now pour the pumpkin batter into the loaf pan and sprinkle the chopped pecans over the top.

5   Place the pan into the hot oven and bake for 65-75 minutes until golden and a toothpick inserted into the centre of the loaf comes out clean.

6   Remove from the oven and place the pan on a wire rack to cool completely before removing the pumpkin bread from the pan.

7   You can store the bread in an airtight container on the counter top for 3-4 days.

CALORIES
184

CARBS
29G

PROTEIN
2G

FAT
7G

CORIANDER & MINT DIP

Impress your guests!
A delightfully elegant snack where sweet meets savoury.

 5 MINS SERVES 10

INGREDIENTS

125g natural yogurt

3 tbsp fresh lemon juice

15g coriander

15g mint leaves

1 jalapeño, sliced
(optional)

2 tsp. root ginger, sliced

1 garlic clove

½ tsp salt

½ tsp sugar

METHOD

1   Place all the ingredients into a blender or food processor and blitz until smooth.

2   Place in an airtight container and store in the refrigerator for up to 4 days.

Perfect with the Tandoori Bowl (see recipe on pg43).

CALORIES
21

CARBS
2G

PROTEIN
1G

FAT
1G

SWEET POTATO HUMMUS

A healthy, filling dip to accompany your savoury snacks or meals.

 10 MINS **SERVES 8**

INGREDIENTS

250g chickpeas, drained

255g sweet potato, mashed

4 tbsp tahini

½ tsp smoked paprika

1 garlic clove, minced

METHOD

1   Place all the ingredients to a high speed blender or food processor and blitz smooth.

2   Serve as a dip.

CALORIES
183

CARBS
16G

PROTEIN
5G

FAT
9G

Sweet Treats

CHOCOLATE & PEANUT BUTTER ICE CREAM CAKE

5 simple ingredients for this jaw dropping sweet treat, with nearly 10g protein per slice!

 50 MINS   SERVES 8

INGREDIENTS

290g chocolate ice cream (allow to melt to a very soft serve consistency)

155g self raising flour

125g peanut butter

1/2 tsp salt

170g chocolate chips

METHOD

1   Preheat the oven to 175C.

2   Line a 9x5 bread pan with parchment paper and grease with a non-stick spray.

3   Once ice cream is a very soft serve consistency, combine with self raising flour and salt. Mix well until combined.

4   Stir in chocolate chips and pour batter into the pan.

5   Swirl peanut butter into the top of the mix.

6   Bake for 35-40 minutes (Baking times may vary from oven to oven).

7   Allow to cool, slice and serve.

CALORIES
380

CARBS
41G

PROTEIN
9G

FAT
29G

2 INGREDIENT ICE CREAM CAKE

This will blow your mind! The easiest, quickest cake recipe ever!

 10 MINS  SERVES 8

INGREDIENTS

290g ice cream (allow to melt to a very soft serve consistency)

155g self raising flour

Optional
50g sprinkles

METHOD

1   Preheat the oven to 175C.

2   Once ice cream is a very soft serve consistency, combine with self raising flour. Mix well until combined.

3   Line a 9x5 bread pan with parchment paper and grease with a non-stick spray.

4   Pour batter into the pan and spread evenly. Add sprinkles if desired.

5   Bake for 35-40 minutes (baking times may vary from oven to oven).

6   Allow to cool slightly before cutting, serve and enjoy.

Nice served with ice cream!

CALORIES
225

CARBS
39G

PROTEIN
5G

FAT
6G

LEMON BLUEBERRY YOGHURT CAKE

LOW CALORIE

An amazingly scrummy and healthy cake!

 15 MINS **SERVES 12**

INGREDIENTS

330g whole wheat flour or all purpose flour

1½ tsp baking powder

¾ tsp bicarbonate of soda

½ tsp salt

3 tbsp grated lemon zest

1 tbsp coconut oil, melted (alternative if preferred)

3 egg whites, room temperature

1 tbsp vanilla extract

1 tsp stevia (or sugar if preferred)

180g non-fat greek yoghurt

120ml freshly squeezed lemon juice

150ml unsweetened almond milk

210g blueberries

METHOD

1   Preheat the oven to 180°C. Line a loaf tin with baking paper.

2   Add the flour, baking powder, bicarbonate of soda, salt and lemon zest into a medium sized bowl and stir to combine.

3   In a separate bowl, whisk together the coconut oil, egg whites, vanilla extract and stevia. Now add the greek yoghurt to this mixture and stir until there are no large lumps. Next, incorporate the lemon juice and 2 tablespoons of the almond milk.

4   Alternating, add the flour mixture and the remaining milk to the wet ingredients, starting and ending with the flour mixture. Stir until just combined, ideally adding the flour mixture in three equal portions.

5   Reserve 2 tablespoons of blueberries and gently fold the remaining berries into the batter using a spatula.

6   Spread the batter evenly into the prepared tin and delicately press the reserved blueberries into the top.

7   Bake the cake in the hot oven for 45-55 minutes or until the top is firm to the touch, and a toothpick inserted into the centre comes out clean.

8   Remove from the oven and allow the cake to cool in the pan for 10 minutes, before transferring it to a wire rack to cool completely.

9   Store the cake in an airtight container on the counter top for up to 5 days.

CALORIES
154

CARBS
27G

PROTEIN
5G

FAT
3G

Sweet Treats

LOW CALORIE

CHOCOLATE TRUFFLES

Yummy very chocolatey bites!

 15 MINS SERVES 20

INGREDIENTS

200g dark chocolate (traditional, dairy-free, or vegan), finely chopped

100ml oat milk

1 tbsp coconut sugar (or regular sugar if preferred)

1 tsp vanilla extract

2 tbsp cocoa powder

METHOD

1   Place the chocolate into a medium sized heatproof bowl.

2   Add the oat milk, coconut sugar and vanilla extract into a small pot, then bring to the boil over a medium heat.

3   Pour the hot milk over the chocolate, then stir until the chocolate has melted. Cover and refrigerate for 4 hours until the mixture has set.

4   Roll the set mixture into 20 balls and then roll in the cocoa powder.

5   Store in an airtight container in the refrigerator for up to 4 days.

CALORIES
66

CARBS
6G

PROTEIN
1G

FAT
4G

CHEESECAKE STUFFED STRAWBERRIES

A quick healthy sweet snack.

 10 MINS SERVES 2

INGREDIENTS

12 strawberries
60g quark
1 tbsp light cream cheese
1 tbsp honey
1 tsp vanilla extract
1 digestive biscuit, crushed

METHOD

1 Remove the tops of the strawberries and with a shape knife cut out the centre of the strawberries.

2 Mix together the quark, cream cheese, honey and vanilla extract.

3 Fill the strawberries with the mixture and sprinkle with cracker/biscuit crumbs. Store the strawberries in the refrigerator until ready to serve.

CALORIES
136

CARBS
21G

PROTEIN
5G

FAT
4G

HAZELNUT ENERGY BALLS

A tasty high protein, healthy snack.

 5 MINS SERVES 6

INGREDIENTS

135g hazelnuts

30g 85% dark chocolate

1 tbsp coconut oil
(alternative if preferred)

8 medjool dates, pitted

1 tsp vanilla extract

For decoration:

85g 85% dark chocolate,
melted

10 hazelnuts, chopped

METHOD

1   Preheat the oven to 160°C. Line a baking sheet
with parchment paper.

2   Place the dark chocolate and oil in a small mixing
bowl and melt in the microwave or in a saucepan.

3   In the bowl of a food processor, add the roasted
hazelnuts, pitted medjool dates, vanilla extract and
the melted chocolate/oil mixture.

4   Process for 2-3 minutes, the time required
depends on the power of the food processor.
The mixture is ready when it forms a sticky batter
that comes together. If too dry, blend in an extra
teaspoon of almond milk or water until the dough
sticks together.

5   Refrigerate the dough for 10 minutes in a bowl.

6   Roll 8 even-sized balls, and place on a plate
covered with parchment paper. Decorate the
energy balls with a drizzle of melted chocolate
and chopped hazelnuts.

7   Store the energy balls for up to 10 days in an
airtight container in the refrigerator.

CALORIES
210

CARBS
23G

PROTEIN
3G

FAT
14G

Sweet Treats

CHOCOLATE STRAWBERRY YOGHURT BITES

A healthier alternative to ice cream or high sugar sweet treats!

 10 MINS  SERVES 9

INGREDIENTS

300g strawberries, chopped

250g unsweetened greek yoghurt

1 tbsp honey

170g dark chocolate chips

2 tsp coconut oil

METHOD

1   Line a baking tray with parchment paper.

2   In a bowl, combine strawberries, yoghurt and honey.

3   Spoon the mixture out onto the prepared baking tray, spacing them out evenly.

4   Place the tray in the freezer for about 30 minutes to allow the yoghurt to firm up.

5   In the meantime, melt the chocolate chips and coconut oil in a microwave-safe bowl in 30 second intervals, stirring until smooth and fully melted.

6   Remove the tray from the freezer and using a fork, dip each frozen bite into the melted chocolate until fully coated.

7   Place the coated clusters back on the parchment paper.

8   Optional: sprinkle crushed nuts, dried fruit or crushed salt on top of the bites for added flavour.

9   Return the tray to the freezer for another 15 minutes until the bites are completely set and serve.

CALORIES
142

CARBS
16G

PROTEIN
4G

FAT
7G

LOW CALORIE

CHOCOLATE NO BAKE PEANUT BUTTER BALLS

In under 10 minutes, you can have these ready to go for your weekly snack!

🕐 **10 MINS** 👤 **SERVES 10**

INGREDIENTS

80g oats
85g honey
60g smooth peanut butter
2 tbsp cocoa powder
pinch of salt

METHOD

1 In a medium-size bowl, mix all the ingredients together.

2 Wet hands. Use a tablespoon to scoop the dough and roll between your palms to form balls.

3 Enjoy straight away or allow to chill in the fridge for 1-2 hours and become more firm.

They store in the fridge for up to a week or the freezer for up to 3 months.

CALORIES
93

CARBS
13G

PROTEIN
3G

FAT
4G

PEANUT BUTTER & RASPBERRY JAM COOKIES

Yummy cookies, less than 100 calories each!

 10 MINS **SERVES 20**

INGREDIENTS

120g whole wheat flour (or regular flour)

¾ tsp baking powder

⅛ tsp salt

½ tbsp butter, melted

1 egg white, room temperature

1 tsp vanilla extract

4½ tbsp peanut butter preferably smooth

100g coconut sugar (or white sugar)

140g raspberry jam

METHOD

1 Preheat the oven to 180°C. Line a baking sheet with baking paper.

2 In a medium bowl, mix together the flour, baking powder and salt.

3 In a separate bowl, whisk together the butter, egg white and vanilla extract. Stir in the peanut butter and mix until smooth, then add in the sugar. Add in the flour mixture and stir just until incorporated.

4 Divide the dough into 24 balls and place on the baking sheet.

5 Gently press your thumb or index finger into the centre of each cookie to make a well. Fill the centres of the cookies with the jam.

6 Place the baking sheet into the hot oven and bake for 10-12 minutes. Remove from the oven and set the baking sheet onto a wire rack to cool for 5 minutes, then place the cookies onto the wire rack to cool completely.

CALORIES
91

CARBS
14G

PROTEIN
2G

FAT
3G

Sweet Treats

HIGH PROTEIN

VANILLA PROTEIN PUDDING

A super healthy, sweet high protein dessert.

🕙 **10 MINS**　👤 **SERVES 2**　GF　V

INGREDIENTS

250g greek yogurt
30g vanilla protein powder
2 tsp vanilla extract
1 tsp maple syrup

Toppings:
2 tbsp blueberries
1 banana, sliced
2 tsp hemp seeds (or seeds of choice)

Feel free to top with other berries and seeds!

METHOD

1　Place the Greek yogurt, protein powder, vanilla extract and maple syrup into a bowl and stir to combine.

2　To serve, divide the mixture equally between 2 bowls or glasses

3　Top with the blueberries, sliced banana and hemp seeds.

CALORIES
241

CARBS
25G

PROTEIN
25G

FAT
4G

Sweet Treats

LOW CALORIE

BANANA NICE CREAM

An absolute winner for a super healthy summer treat!
Fruit based nice cream!

 10 MINS **SERVES 2**

INGREDIENTS

300g frozen banana slices
(2 large bananas)

2-4 tablespoons almond
milk, unsweetened

METHOD

1 Place frozen banana slices and 2 tablespoons unsweetened almond milk into a high speed food processor or blender

2 Blend on high for 1 - 2 minutes stopping to scrape the sides every so often. Add more milk if necessary

3 Once blended, your nice cream should be soft to serve. Eat immediately or transfer to a parchment-lined bread pan to freeze for later

4 Freeze banana nice cream for 1-2 hours so that it hardens enough to scoop. If it becomes too hard then leave to thaw for a little while first

CALORIES
123

CARBS
31G

PROTEIN
2G

FAT
1G

CARROT & APPLE MUFFINS

Healthy low calorie cakes.

 10 MINS  **SERVES 12**

INGREDIENTS

130g carrots, grated

170g apples, peeled & grated

100g ground almonds

60g raisins

1½ tsp mixed spice

1 tsp ground cinnamon

1 tsp baking powder

75g ricotta cheese

3 eggs

1 tsp vanilla extract

For frosting:

1 tsp vanilla extract

125g cream cheese

2 tsp honey

METHOD

1   Preheat the oven to 180°C. Line a 12-hole muffin tin with small muffin cases.

2   Place all the ingredients for the muffins into a large bowl and beat together with a wooden spoon to form a cake batter.

3   Divide the mixture equally between each of the muffin cases and place the muffin tin into the hot oven.

4   Bake the muffins for 25 minutes, by which time they will be cooked through and a little golden on the top. Remove the muffin cases from the tin and place on a wire rack to cool.

5   While the muffins are cooling, make the frosting, by whipping together the vanilla extract, cream cheese and honey, adding a splash of water to slacken if needed.

6   Once the muffins have cooled completely, spread the cream cheese icing on top.

CALORIES
139

CARBS
11G

PROTEIN
5G

FAT
9G

Sweet Treats

EASY OAT AND CARROT COOKIES

An easy recipe which contributes towards your 5 a day!

 15 MINS SERVES 8

INGREDIENTS

1 medium carrot, grated
100g instant oats
100g whole-grain flour
1 tsp baking powder
1 tsp ground cinnamon
3 tbsp coconut oil, melted
1 egg
1 tsp vanilla extract
75ml maple syrup

METHOD

1   Preheat oven to 170°C. Mix the oats, flour, baking powder and cinnamon in a bowl.

2   In a separate bowl, whisk together, the egg melted and cooled oil, vanilla extract and maple syrup. Fold in the dry ingredients and mix well.

3   Add in the finely grated carrot and mix again.

4   Spoon the mixture (1 heaped tablespoon per cookie) onto a baking tray lined with paper and shape into rounds, leaving space between each cookie as they will spread slightly while cooking.

5   Place in the preheated oven and bake for 12-15 minutes until slightly browned. Remove from the oven and allow to cool completely before serving.

CALORIES
181

CARBS
26G

PROTEIN
3G

FAT
7G

Sweet Treats

CHOCOLATE NUTTY APPLE POPS

A nutritious sweet treat using apple, nuts and dark chocolate.

 15 MINS SERVES 6

INGREDIENTS

1 large apple

60g cup smooth peanut butter

3 tbsp dark chocolate, melted

75g peanut halves

3 tbsp honey

METHOD

1 Mix the peanut butter and honey together to make a caramel. Spread the peanuts on a small plate.

2 Slice the apple into 2-3 slices either side of the stem (about 1/2 an inch wide to ensure the stock doesn't break it).

3 Use a knife to make a small slit at the bottom of each slice.

4 Insert a lolly stick into each slice.

5 Add 1 tbsp caramel to the top of each apple and use a spoon to spread to cover the top.

6 Press the caramel side of the apple onto the plate to cover with peanuts.

7 Dip in melted chocolate. You may need a spoon to cover the apple.

8 Place on a baking tray lined with parchment paper and refrigerate to harden.

CALORIES
243

CARBS
22G

PROTEIN
6G

FAT
18G

HEALTHY APPLE CRUMBLE

A deliciously warming dessert.

 10 MINS SERVES 10

INGREDIENTS

For the crumble:

120g rolled oats

65g whole wheat flour (or all purpose if preferred)

2 tsp ground cinnamon

4 tbsp maple syrup

3 tbsp coconut oil, melted (swap for butter if preferred)

For the filling:

710g red apple, diced

2 tbsp cornstarch

1½ tsp ground cinnamon

⅛ tsp ground nutmeg

METHOD

1   Preheat the oven to 180°C. Grease an 8x8-inch pan with non-stick cooking spray.

2   To make the crumble, place the rolled oats, flour and ground cinnamon into a large bowl and mix together. Make a well in the centre and pour in the maple syrup and melted coconut oil. Stir again until well combined.

3   To make the filling, toss the diced apples (no need to peel the apples) with the cornstarch, cinnamon, and nutmeg in a large bowl, ensuring the apples are completely coated.

4   Transfer the apples to the earlier prepared pan and gently press down with a spatula. Sprinkle over the crumble topping.

5   Place the pan into the hot oven and bake for 50-60 minutes or until the apples are tender.

6   Remove the pan from the oven and set on a wire rack and cool to room temperature. Now refrigerate the crumble for at least 3 hours to allow the apple juices to fully thicken, before serving.

CALORIES
182

CARBS
32G

PROTEIN
1G

FAT
5G

Sweet Treats

GOLDEN MILK SMOOTHIE

Delicious, filling, high protein breakfast or snack.

 5 MINS SERVES 1

INGREDIENTS

165g mango, diced, frozen
½ banana, frozen
240ml almond milk, unsweetened
1 scoop 25g vanilla protein powder (of choice)
1 tbsp cashew butter
1 tsp honey
½ ground tumeric
½ tsp ground cinnamon
¼ tsp ground ginger

METHOD

Place all the ingredients in a high speed blender and blitz until smooth.

Serve immediately.

CALORIES
388

CARBS
50G

PROTEIN
28G

FAT
11G

BLUEBERRY & POMEGRANATE SMOOTHIE

A quick, nutritious snack.

 5 MINS SERVES 2

INGREDIENTS

225g frozen blueberries
240ml pomegranate juice
190g Greek yogurt
120ml water
1 banana
1 tsp. honey

METHOD

Place all the ingredients into a high speed blender and blend until smooth and creamy.

Divide the smoothie between 2 glasses and serve immediately.

CALORIES
268

CARBS
54G

PROTEIN
11G

FAT
3G

PIÑA COLADA PROTEIN SMOOTHIE

High protein tasty snack.

 10 MINS SERVES 2

INGREDIENTS

400ml can low fat coconut milk
1 banana
100g frozen pineapple
100g frozen mango
50g vanilla protein powder

METHOD

Add the coconut milk, banana, pineapple, mango and protein powder to a blender and blend on high until smooth.

Divide between 2 glasses and serve immediately.

CALORIES
320

CARBS
32G

PROTEIN
21G

FAT
13G

BETTER SLEEP SMOOTHIE

A dreamy bed time smoothie.

 5 MINS  SERVES 2

INGREDIENTS

150g cottage cheese
1 banana, frozen
2 tbsp walnuts
50g cherries, frozen
2 tbsp rolled oats
90ml chamomile tea, chilled
1 tsp ground cinnamon
1 tbsp honey

METHOD

Place all the ingredients into a high speed blender and blitz until smooth. Pour into a glasses and serve immediately.

Divide between 2 glasses and serve immediately.

CALORIES
237

CARBS
32G

PROTEIN
11G

FAT
9G

ISBN **9 798870 719238**

Written by Kate Healey-Stapleton.
Designed by Joanna Humphrey.

www.legsbumsandbubbas.com

🔵 **kate_fitness.for.mums**

❶ **Legs, Bums & Bubbas**

Printed in Great Britain
by Amazon

38501861R00082